FARNBOROUGH PAST

The last meeting of Farnborough Urban District Council in 1974, when the Chairman was Mr. G.J. Woolgar.

FARNBOROUGH PAST

Jo Gosney

Phillimore

2001

Published by
PHILLIMORE & CO. LTD.
Shopwyke Manor Barn, Chichester, West Sussex

ISBN 1 86077 186 6

Printed and bound in Great Britain by
BIDDLES LTD.
Guildford, Surrey

Contents

List of Illustrations

Frontispiece: The last meeting of Farnborough Urban District Council in 1974

Acknowledgements

The author wishes to acknowledge the following for permission to reproduce illustrations:

Mr. R. Allum, 28, 73, 78, 79, 129, 130; Mrs. J. Bailey née Spreadborough, 141; Mr. R.K. Blencowe, 118; Mrs. B.A. Candy, 135; Mrs. J. Chapman, 53, 84; Mr. L. Coleman, 10; Crown Copyright, 108; Mr. J. Darwin, 68; Mrs. Jessie Dyke née Angel, 138; Mr. M. Edgoose, 93; Mrs. M. Gale, 60; Mr. R. Gibbens, 139; Hampshire Record Office, 12 (ref: IM45/9/3), 18 (ref: 50M63/C98), 29 (ref: 30M73/F10), 33 (ref: 15M82/E/T4), front endpaper (ref: 1M45/20), back endpaper (ref: PL2/2/3); Mr. Bill Harman, 114, 115; Mr. H. Holloway, 95, 100, 147; Mrs. A. Joyce, 55; Mr. T.J. Lawrence, 98; Mr. A. Lunn, 37; Dr. and Mrs. A. MacAdam, 56; Mr. R.D. McLaurin, 131; Mrs. N. Martin née Landymore, 87, 119; Mrs. M. May, 43; Miss C. Osment, 109;   Public Record Office, Kew, 17 (ref: WH12/10790), 24 (ref: ZPER/12/24); Mr. G. Robinson, 106; Salesian School, 105, 132; Mr. J. Shepherd, 122; Mr. D.E. Treadgold, 69; Mr. P. Trevaskis and the Bus Interest Group, 23, 71; Mr. P. Vickery, 41, 97; Mrs. M. Waters, 133; Mrs. W. Watts, 31; Mrs. M. Woods, 80.

The author is grateful for the permission of Her Majesty The Queen to make use of the excerpts from Queen Victoria's Diary reproduced in Chapter Five.

Thanks are also due to the staff at Farnborough Library, Farnham Museum, Hampshire Record Office, Rushmoor Borough Council, Janet Smith of the North East Hampshire Archaeological Society, and Ian Maine of the Aldershot Military Museum for their assistance with research; and to Jim Gaines and my ever supportive husband Michael for their photographic help.

Introduction

Mention Farnborough and most people think of aeroplanes. However, aeroplanes only span a century, whereas the documented history of Farnborough spans more than a millennium.

Much of the early development was influenced by outside factors such as the construction of the railways and the arrival of the army in Aldershot, but underlying these was always a backbone of village life. Despite the rapid expansion of the last 150 years, that core element is still evident today from the local family names which can be traced back through the generations.

Fifty years ago, Brian Vesey-Fitzgerald in his book *Hampshire and The Isle of Wight* wrote of Farnborough: 'Once there was a lovely church there ... it has been greatly enlarged ... there is another church built by the Empress Eugénie ... and an inn called the Dick Inn ... that is about all the history you can dig up about the place.'

Through the pages of this book I shall endeavour to illustrate that the past in Farnborough should not be dismissed so hastily. Some of the stories are anecdotal but much has been gleaned from research in various archives around the country. All that, together with many photographs borrowed from local people, will, I hope, give you an insight into Farnborough Past.

Chapter One

Ancient History

There are very few relics from prehistoric times in Farnborough although its position half-way between the South Coast and London would lead you to believe it should be otherwise. Ancient tracks and roads crossing this north-eastern corner of Hampshire have revealed disappointingly little.

The presence of tumuli indicates pre-historic burial mounds but no other traces of earlier settlements have been discovered. One tumulus is in Albert Road and does not appear to have been excavated. The other is on Cockadobby Hill, at the Queen's Roundabout on the A325. That tumulus was excavated in the 1830s by Mr. Edward Greene, who founded early schools on the borders with Cove, but no records of his findings exist. He is believed to have buried examples of local pottery, coins of

the realm and a copy of *The Times* newspaper for possible future archaeologists to discover. However, two later excavations on the site revealed neither Mr. Greene's relics nor any other interesting finds. In 1902 a memorial was erected nearby, dedicated to the memory of an unknown soldier who died in the Boer War. The name Cockadobby is said to have been derived from the Old English word for a dobby or goblin, which only adds to the mystery and legend about its origin. A third tumulus is thought to have been near the present Fire Station on Lynchford Road, and although shown on a very early estate map it is not shown on subsequent Ordnance Survey maps. Possibly it disappeared beneath the hurriedly erected huts in North Camp at the time of the Crimean War.

1 Cockadobby Hill shortly after the memorial to an unknown soldier in the Boer War had been erected.

2 St Peter's parish church, showing the lych-gate erected in 1907 in memory of the Holt family, and the mounting stones on the right-hand side.

At the entrance to the parish church, there are two large flat stones which have long been the subject of conjecture. Credence could certainly be given to the story that they were used as mounting stones in the days of horse-drawn travel for they are ideally positioned. Their origin could well reach back to Saxon times. They may be Ice-Age deposits. Similar but smaller stones were found near Cockadobby Hill in the early 1900s.

Occasional finds of antiquities have been recorded over the years. In the early 1920s a number of Roman coins were found in the area of the Manor House Farm, and in 1941 some Greek coins were dug up in another part of Farnborough Park. Some coins were also found in High Street but the present where-abouts of all these finds is not known. Jessie Challacombe in her *Jottings from a Farnborough Notebook* recounts that, in the mid-1800s, when the Rev. Clayton was living in the old Rectory, Mr. Greene carried out some excavations beside Rectory Road and discovered 'an ancient urn, broken pottery, the bones of an ape and a skeleton of a stag as well as a quantity of ashes

and a valuable blue bead'. These supposedly went to the British Museum but now appear to have become lost in the mists of time. Therefore, lacking ancient remains, we have to look to the written word to form a picture of the very early history.

The Manor of Farnborough was in the somewhat isolated north-eastern part of the Hundred of Crondal (nowadays spelt Crondall), in the north of the Shire of Southampton. F.J. Baigent, in his publication in 1891 of *A Collection of Records and Documents relating to the Hundred of Crondal*, explains that

> The Hundred of Crondal comprises a large tract of land extending over an area of nearly 29,000 acres, and was given to the Cathedral Church of Winchester as far back as Anglo-Saxon days towards the support of the Bishop and monks. It was formed previous to the Conquest into an ecclesiastical district and placed entirely under the supervision of the Rector of Crondal, with the exception of a small portion on the east side containing about 2,300 acres, which was taken out of its area and constituted a separate parish—of Farnborough.

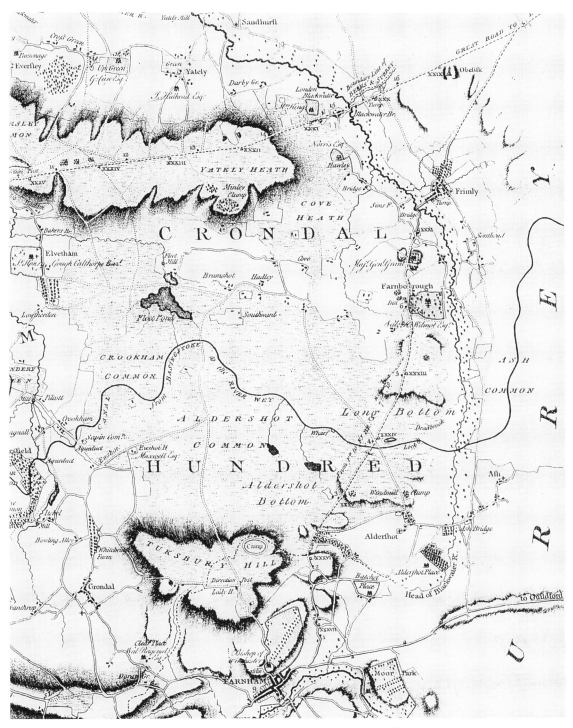

3 A map dated 1791 showing the Hundred of Crondal (today spelt Crondall). The milestones on the turnpike road are clearly marked in Roman numerals.

The parish forms a triangle bounded on the east by the River Blackwater and on the west by the villages of Cove and Hawley, with the southern limit just north of the Basingstoke Canal.

In an English translation of the Domesday survey of 1086, ordered by William the Conqueror, we are told:

> Odin of Windsor holds 3 hides of this manor from the Bishop in FARNBOROUGH. Alwin held it jointly from the Bishop; he could not go whither he would. Now in lordship 1 plough; 7 villagers and 4 smallholders with 3 ploughs. 5 slaves; a mill at 10d; meadow, 3 acres; woodland at 6 pigs.
> Value before 1066 and now 60s; when acquired 40s.

Farnborough has been spelt in a number of different ways through the ages. Ferneberg, Ferneberga, Farnburghe, Farenberg, Frembrough, Farnborowe and Farnboro have all been recorded but it settled down to the more familiar spelling of Farnborough in about the 17th century. Meaning 'Hill of Ferns', it is derived from Ferne, meaning the plant, with Borough being an alternative form of the word 'barrow', a hill of some form, either natural or artificial, such as a tumulus.

According to another important historical work, the *Victoria County History of Hampshire* published in the early 1900s, the next reference to Farnborough is in 1230 when Stephen de Farnborough is acknowledged to be 'the true patron of the Church'. It is not known when the church was dedicated but the records show an almost unbroken succession of rectors since 1290.

The building of the parish church of St Peter dates from around 1200. The circular plan of the original churchyard would seem to be strong evidence that an earlier Saxon church may have been built on the site. The north and west walls of the present nave remain from that early church, together with a small chancel and a crypt under the greater part of the nave.

4   The parish church *c*.1900, before the north and south transepts were built.

5 Thirteenth-century wall paintings discovered in the parish church in 1881.

In 1881, whilst refurbishment was being under-taken in the church, some 13th-century paintings were discovered depicting St Eugenia, St Agnes and St Mary Magdalene. The painting of St Eugenia is particularly interesting as it is believed to be the only representation of her in this country. A daughter of Philip, Duke of Alexandria, who was the Governor of Rome under Egypt, she converted many to Christianity and was eventually martyred by beheading.

The north doorway is also from that early period although the age of the actual door is unknown. There were few windows in this tiny church in Norman times, so the gloomy interior may well have helped to preserve the paintings. Substantial alterations took place in the 15th century but only the porch and one of the windows from that period remain. The 17th-century tower is made of wood over a framework of what are thought to be ship's timbers. Inside the tower are eight bells, four of which date back to the 1600s. Built on a hill, the church is said to have been the inspi-ration for the hymn, 'There is a green hill far away', written by Mrs. Alexander. She was sister of the Rev. Clayton and often visited her brother at the old Rectory.

The original churchyard, which was closed to burials in 1859, was completely encircled by a low walled embankment, only part of which survives today. Further enlargement and major alterations took place early in the 20th century, and a new community church hall was added

in 1999. This ancient church in its tranquil setting has survived the ravages of time and is a visible link with every chapter in the history of Farnborough.

The succession of the manor continues through Henry de Farnborough in 1243, and John de Farnborough in 1316, followed by Amice de Farnborough who held it in 1346. There follows a period of uncertainty when in 1353 John de Sherborne, who appears to have acquired the manor, fell into debt and traded it to a creditor, William de Bricklesworth. By 1428 Joan atte More had one part of the manor, the remainder being in the hands of William Dawtrey, who subsequently split it further among his heirs.

In 1535 Richard Norton, having married into the Dawtrey family, left one part to his son John, who probably purchased all the other parts, as on his death he left the whole manor to his son, Sir Richard Norton. When he died in 1619 it was inherited by his son Richard, who sold it on to John Godson and Edward Dickenson, both of Odiham. Edward Dickinson became lord of the manor in 1619 but in 1630 John Godson is recorded as having held court as lord of the manor.

A few years later the manor was in the hands of the Annesley family and became one of the seats of the Earls of Anglesey. The first Lord of Anglesey, Arthur Annesley, is found in the parish records in 1661. Five of the Earls of Anglesey are shown in the burial records, the last being in 1737. In 1768 Henry Wilmot appears as lord of the manor, succeeded by his son Valentine Henry Wilmot in 1794.

Once again the manor became the subject of a debt settlement and it was forfeited to George Pindar in 1817. A gap appears in the ownership until George Morant purchased it in 1848. He remained lord of the manor until his death in 1875 when the manor was sold, but the title lord of the manor remained with his trustees until it was sold to Richard Eve, an Aldershot solicitor, in 1885. Mr. Eve died in 1900 and the title was purchased by Mrs. M. Holt, of Farnborough Grange. Her son, Harold Edwin Sherwin Holt, inherited the title on her death in 1904.

Apart from farming, the only early industry in this area on the borders of Surrey and Hampshire was pottery making, which flourished during the 14th century. There were two types of clay used locally, a very fine light-coloured clay from the Reading Beds found near Farnham, and a coarser variety of London Clay found in localised outcrops on the common at Cove. The pottery produced in this area was called Border Ware and would have been for local domestic use as well as being transported by cart to the London markets.

In Tudor times there was a great increase in demand for domestic utensils, and the local potters responded by producing a type of green-glazed ware for drinking vessels. Examples of the local Border Ware have been found in the royal palaces at Hampton Court and Nonsuch. An earlier royal use is recorded in *Building in England* by L.F. Salzman, who tells us that 'in 1391 over 200 earthenware pots were taken by cart from Farnborough to Windsor for use in

6   The Manor House in the 1920s, just before it was turned into a nursing home.

7 Seventeenth-century pottery. A costrel (portable flask) and a pipkin (cooking pot) found at the site in the grounds of Farnborough Hill.

the King's baths'. Another reference to potters is in a document of 1649 witnessed by a Richard Milton, potter, of Farnborough.

The majority of the Border Ware sites are recorded in nearby Cove, but in 1967 a site was discovered beneath a fallen tree in the grounds of Farnborough Hill. Extensive excavations resulted in the discovery that a wide variety of good quality domestic utensils were made there. Many items appeared to have accidental splashing of different coloured glaze on them, which could indicate a shared use of the kilns by a number of local potters. A further indication of a substantial output was the large amount of sherds or pottery waste found. Some of the recovered items are held by the Aldershot Military Museum. It is thought this site was active until about the late 17th century, although there was another pottery in the village which continued production until the mid-1800s.

Chapter Two

The Manorial Years

When the manor came into the hands of the Annesley family, in the early 1660s, the house was known as Farnborough Place. It is believed that the present house was redesigned by Sir Christopher Wren, as it has some of Wren's features. The association was made because Arthur Annesley, the first Earl of Anglesey, was Lord Privy Seal at the time when Wren rebuilt St Paul's Cathedral. Although only one of the Annesley country seats, it was obviously a favourite, and the surrounding parkland was laid out with numerous trees, some of which survive today. John Mackey, in his chronicle *A Journey Through all England* published in 1722, wrote that on his journey from Egham to Farnham he traversed through totally barren wasteland except for 'a hunting seat of the Earl of Anglesey's called Farnborough which makes the better appearance standing in so coarse a country, and being very well planted with trees'.

Farnborough had always been dominated by the lord of the manor, who was for many years the sole landowner. This situation gradually changed in the latter half of the 18th century at just about the time the manor came into the possession of the Wilmot family.

Henry Wilmot was a well-known solicitor in Gray's Inn, London. He entertained lavishly at Farnborough Place and was frequently visited by Sir Joshua Reynolds and David Garrick. Henry's wife, Sarah, reputedly a beautiful woman, was also very popular and there is a glowing memorial to her in the church.

8 Aerial view of the church and the Manor House (far right) in the 1920s.

9 Memorial to Hoppy the cat set in a garden wall at the Manor House.

Following one of his visits to Farnborough, Sir Joshua Reynolds paid her the compliment of painting her portrait.

David Garrick's visits are remembered for his poem dedicated to a cat. His words were for many years visible on a memorial set in a garden wall at Farnborough Place, beneath which was a profile of the cat and her kittens. Sadly this memorial disappeared when building work was being carried out in the 1960s and a recently discovered photograph only shows the cats' profiles, but the words are recorded in Jessie Challacombe's book:

> Nine lives in sin and sorrow spent,
> Finished their course beneath this stone;
> Here lies a wretch on blood so bent
> She like Medea, spilt her own.
> Death saw here deeds, and justice grew
> To have a rival in his blade,
> With envy saw the heaps she slew,
> And all the havoc she had made.
> In rage the fatal dart he drives,
> Not her nine lives his hunger pall,
> Had Hoppy's every hair been lives,
> Death had a stomach for them all.

In the mid–1920s Farnborough Place was sold to become a nursing home, followed by a period as a hotel, particularly frequented by RAF and army officers. It was occupied by Power Jets in 1950 and used by the International Turbine School and Sir Frank Whittle, the pioneer of the jet engine. In the late 1950s it was threatened by demolition but, fortunately, this historic building, which once dominated the lives of the villagers, was saved to take on the mantle of shaping the lives of our children. St Peter's School transferred into Farnborough Place in 1962.

The main entrance to Farnborough Place was originally a wide carriageway sweeping up the hill from the Farnborough Road. Visitors drove through tall metal gates guarded by a small lodge on either side. Built around the beginning of the 19th century, the lodges were occupied by the gardeners on the estate. George Godfrey was a gardener around the 1860s and his grandson recalls being told that the family lived in one lodge and slept in the other. Soon after the estate was sold in the 1920s, the lodges

10   Entrance lodges to the Manor House.

came down to make way for houses. Great sadness was expressed in the local press at the loss of these historic cottages. Nevertheless the demolition materials may still be around somewhere in the town as it was reported that the crushed stone was to be used to construct a local road!

The administration of the manor's affairs was undertaken in a manorial court called a Court Baron. Regular Courts Baron were held until well into the 19th century and were presided over by the Steward or Bailiff who was the representative of the lord of the manor. Some records of these courts survive from as early as the 16th century, the earliest ones generally being in Latin. They give an insight into use of the land and the way in which the lord of the manor controlled and influenced the lives and fortunes of the tenants. All the chief tenants of the manor had to attend and, if they failed to do so without a reasonable excuse, paid a stipulated fine. In the early years

these courts were held in the Manor House itself, or in the Manor Farm House which stood just behind the houses which now form Barnes Close, off Rectory Road. Mentioned in early 16th-century documents, the Manor Farm House afforded substantial accommodation for the Steward as befitted an estate employee of considerable importance. When sold by the main estate, in 1904, it was still being used as the Estate Office.

Tenants would pay their dues for such privileges as letting a hog out on to the common, but they were fined 2s. 6d. if the hog did not wear a ring in its nose. Privileged tenants profited from the waste land by such activities as cutting of furze and digging up loam and sand. However, they were heavily fined if they took such pickings out of the parish. Certain trees could be felled, but not oak, ash and elm, as this was the prerogative of the lord of the manor. Tenants caught disobeying this custom were fined twice the value

Farnborough, Hants.

32 Miles from London on the L. & S. W. Railway Main Line.

Particulars, Plan and Conditions of Sale

OF THE

Third Portion of the Very Valuable and Desirable Freehold Property

KNOWN AS THE

FARNBOROUGH PARK ESTATE

COMPRISING :

The Manor Farm, of about 4 acres in extent,

AND

Numerous Plots of Building Land, of convenient situation and area.

FOR SALE BY AUCTION

ON THE

MANOR FARM, RECTORY ROAD, FARNBOROUGH, HANTS.

On WEDNESDAY, 12th OCTOBER, 1904,

At 3 o'clock p.m.,

By direction of G. H. BLOIS ELLIOTT, Esq. (the Owner).

Particulars, Plan and Conditions of Sale may be obtained of—

Messrs. MERRIMAN, PIKE & MERRIMAN, Solicitors, 3 Mitre Court, Temple, E.C. ; and

6 Great Winchester Street, E.C. ; and at

THE FARNBOROUGH PARK ESTATE OFFICE,

Manor Farm, Farnborough, Hants.

11   Sale particulars of Farnborough Park Estate.

Manor of Farnborough,

IN THE COUNTY OF SOUTHAMPTON.

Notice is hereby given,

That the General Court Baron and Customary Court of **George Morant, Esq.**, Lord of the said Manor, will be held in and for the said Manor, at the **Tumble Down Dick Inn**, on Wednesday, the 18th day of June next, at 12 o'clock at noon precisely, when and where all persons owing suit and service, claiming admittance to any hereditaments holden of the said Manor, or having any other business to transact at the said Court, are requested to attend, and the respective tenants are desired not to fail paying their Quit rents.

Dated this 24th day of May, 1862.

GEO. W. WRAY,
STEWARD.

1, Verulam Buildings, Gray's Inn,
London.

12   Notice of Court Baron to be held in June 1862. Inns were often the venue for Courts and Inquests because they usually had the facilities to accommodate large numbers of people. There was also the added bonus of refreshments being near to hand.

of the tree. In 1803 one tenant erected a fence and gates around his land thus preventing the lord of the manor from exercising his tree-felling rights. A solicitor's opinion was sought and he ruled that the lord of the manor could only enter if the timber was going to be used to repair the mansion house.

Whenever a property changed hands, either by default, through not paying the rent, or on the decease of the tenant, the steward received a fee of 2s. per transaction. The new owner had then to present himself at the Court Baron so that the changeover could be recorded.

In 1763 a will was presented whereby Ann Shorter left 20s. per year for the poor of Farnborough to purchase bread. She also had property in Cove, and left 10s. per year for the poor of Cove for similar purchases. In 1769 an agreement between Henry Wilmot and the churchwardens allowed him to exchange some ground in the churchyard in order to extend the garden of the Manor

House. In return he offered to extend the wall surrounding the churchyard and help with its upkeep. The churchwardens agreed but not before establishing that no graves were to be disturbed. Although this was a church matter, it had to come before the Court Baron for ratification.

The size of the Manor Estate had been considerably reduced when Henry Wilmot took over, and it was at this time that General Francis Grant became the owner of Windmill Hill, when his wife, Katherine Sophia, inherited it from the 3rd Earl of Annesley. Dorothy Mostyn, in her book *The History of a House* (the story of Farnborough Hill), has written that between 1768 and 1774 a windmill was erected on the summit of Windmill Hill. Certainly the site of the windmill is referred to in the Enclosure Award of 1812 as 'the land whereon a wind-mill formerly stood', and an indenture of sale of the Manor in 1619 states that there were 'fishings, windmills, and water-mills in Farn-borough Manor'.

General Grant died in 1781, and on the death of his widow in 1806 his son James Ludovick Grant inherited the property. Although he was a serving officer in the navy, he had lived at Windmill Hill for most of his life. The title deeds state that in or about 1808 he demolished the old house, situated on the western side of the hill near the turnpike road, and that the estate was greatly enlarged by

> ... the erection of a commodious messuage or dwelling house with suitable coach houses stables and outhouses and also from time to time laid open an annexe to the last mentioned messuage and land the several freehold and copyhold lands acquired by purchase allotment and exchange hereinbefore mentioned made various alterations and improvements therein by the prostration of buildings and various plantations and new fences and enclosures, the whole of which is now usually called or known by the name of Farnborough Hill Estate.

Prior to the early enclosure acts of the late 1700s, much of the land in the country was cultivated under the strip-farming system whereby farmers owned many strips of land which were not necessarily contiguous. Enclosure grouped together landholdings and fields into more manageable farming areas, and in the 18th century this did happen to some extent in Farnborough, but of more local significance was the Enclosure Act of 1811 which appointed an independent Commissioner to survey the land, ascertain ownership and apportion the various plots as fairly as possible, awarding compensation by way of exchange of lands for various rights on the common land.

The Commissioner was George Smallpiece, from Stoke near Guildford, who appointed Job Smallpiece, a land surveyor, to undertake the survey and draw up the plans and apportionments. This survey, notes of the awards and its accompanying map have survived and are an invaluable guide to the landowners, tenants, field names and road directions of the period. It also records the acreage, linear measurement and responsibility for erection and maintenance of fences and boundaries and ditches.

There were 12 carriage roads or carriage-ways recorded on the survey, apart from the London to Winchester turnpike (now Farnborough Road). Two of them were public roads, which were maintained by the parish, and the remaining 10 were private carriage roads giving access to the owners or occupiers of specific properties. One of the public roads led from Coleford Bridge 'in a westerly direction across the London Turnpike Road and from thence continuing in its ancient track into the tithing of Cove', following the ancient road-way used by ecclesiastical travellers from Chertsey Abbey across the Blackwater River on their way to their church properties near Odiham. Today we know these ways as Rectory Road (formerly Dog Kennel Lane, deriving its name from the kennels where the lord of the manor kept his hunting dogs) and, across the roundabout, Victoria Road (formerly Cove Road or New Road). The other public road led from the turnpike near the 'round butt, proceeding in an eastward and straight direction towards the Parish of Ash at Lynch Ford' and is now known as Lynchford Road. The 'round butt' referred to Cockadobby.

Some ancient field names have survived in roads today such as Lye Copse Avenue,

Greatfield Road, and Sand Hill on the Grange Estate but, set in their present semi-urban situations, it is almost impossible to envisage their earlier use. These fields are more accurately recorded on the 1842 Tithe map, where a legend identifies field numbers with the names, owners and uses of the land.

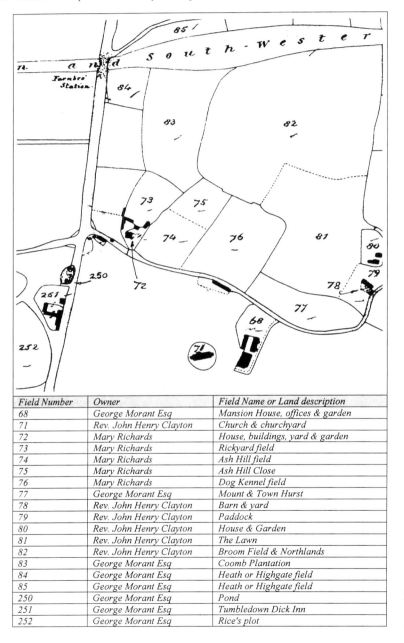

Field Number	Owner	Field Name or Land description
68	George Morant Esq	Mansion House, offices & garden
71	Rev. John Henry Clayton	Church & churchyard
72	Mary Richards	House, buildings, yard & garden
73	Mary Richards	Rickyard field
74	Mary Richards	Ash Hill field
75	Mary Richards	Ash Hill Close
76	Mary Richards	Dog Kennel field
77	George Morant Esq	Mount & Town Hurst
78	Rev. John Henry Clayton	Barn & yard
79	Rev. John Henry Clayton	Paddock
80	Rev. John Henry Clayton	House & Garden
81	Rev. John Henry Clayton	The Lawn
82	Rev. John Henry Clayton	Broom Field & Northlands
83	George Morant Esq	Coomb Plantation
84	George Morant Esq	Heath or Highgate field
85	George Morant Esq	Heath or Highgate field
250	George Morant Esq	Pond
251	George Morant Esq	Tumbledown Dick Inn
252	George Morant Esq	Rice's plot

13 Extract from Tithe map 1842, and table showing field and land details.

14   Sinehurst Farm, Hawley Lane, early 1960s.

Highgate Lane was formerly Heathgate Lane, reflecting a time when the lane from the old village joined the turnpike road at the edge of the heath, beyond which lay the village of Cove. Sine Close reminds us of Sinehurst Farm, which was on a nearby bend in the Hawley Lane. The *Victoria County History* relates that

> Synehurst Farm, in the north of the parish near the Surrey border, is called the manor of Synehurst in 16th-century records. It probably had its origin in the lands in Synehurst which Henry de Farnborough, lord of the manor of Farnborough granted to Osbert de Burstowe in 1259 to hold of him and his heirs for rent of 3s. and suit at the court of Farnborough twice a year. It was acquired by John Norton, lord of the manor of Farnborough, in the middle of the 16th century, and was sold with that manor by the description of the messuage or farm called Sindhurst with appurtenances in Farnborough ...

Hawley Lane led from Hawley into the turnpike just south of Frimley Bridge. An ancient route, it brought travellers from the north west, or from Reading, Blackwater and Hawley, through the old part of the village, now known as Farnborough Street, across Coleford Bridge and on towards Guildford and the South Coast. The crossing of the River Blackwater at Coleford Bridge was probably an important factor in the establishment of a settlement in Farnborough.

At the junction of Farnborough Road and Ship Lane, leading to Farnborough Street, lies *The Ship* inn, which is believed to have derived its name from being built of timbers from a ship called the *Royal Anne*. It is called *The Ship* in the parish records in 1771, when the parish rate was paid by Thomas Hunt. However, it is also referred to as *The Royal Anne* in the manorial records of January 1811, when John Mayne is shown as the tenant. Equally confusing is the fact that, in April 1811, Thomas Wooldridge, the tenant who took over from John Mayne, and William Belsher Parfett were parties to an agreement which names it *The*

15   *The Ship* inn in the 1970s.

Ship. The deeds show that the Simonds family, who owned Simonds Brewery, purchased it in 1856, and the transaction then confirms that the property 'now known as The Ship was formerly The Royal Anne'.

In 1860 a field behind *The Ship*, next to the River Blackwater, was the venue for an illegal bare knuckle prize fight between Tom Sayers, Champion of England, and an American, John Heenan. This 'secret' boxing match was remarkably well publicised, with special trains being run from London Bridge. At 3 a.m. on 17 April, London Bridge station was crowded with travellers who happily purchased their tickets at 5s. a time knowing nothing of their destination other than it would be beyond the clutches of the Metropolitan Police. At 4.30 a.m. the first of two trains departed with its excited passengers, who included titled gentry, high ranking military officers, justices of the peace and brethren of the cloth as well as those of the populace who could afford the price of a ticket.

For the first 16 miles of the journey towards the South Coast, the train was followed closely by the police but, once out of the metropolitan area, it travelled unhindered through the countryside. At Reigate it turned onto the Guildford–Reading line and the destination eventually became apparent when it reached this conveniently open spot, right next to the Surrey and Hampshire borders. The strategic position at the back of *The Ship* had been selected to enable the contestants to make a quick exit across the border in the event of a raid by the local police.

Well over twelve hundred people had arrived by train and the number was soon

16   An engraving of the Championship Prize Fight of 1860 from a book of prints published in America by Currier & Ives. Tom Sayers, the All England Champion, retained the title in a fight lasting nearly two and a half hours despite the challenger's advantage of 4 ½ inches in height and 40lb. in weight.

swelled by local inhabitants including many from the Army Camp, which one visitor observed 'was practically deserted thereby proving that the locale chosen was indeed a happy one'. Some residents today still recount the tales that their grandparents told them about the event.

At the centre of the parish, in the direction of Farnham, what we know today as Sycamore Road was called 'Sickmoor Lane'. This led to Sickmoor Farm, an ancient farmstead in three acres of very poor, marshy soil. The farm is mentioned in the court rolls as being in the tenancy of Thomas Searle in 1781, when he paid rates to the parish. Possibly taking its name from *sick* or *sitch*, describing a piece of low-lying marshy land, the farmhouse is shown on older maps as being sited in what is now King George V playing fields. These playing fields are on the side of a hill, originally waste land called Sickmore Hill.

Opposite Sickmoor Lane was another carriageway leading in a westerly direction. Although once nearly 20ft. wide, it has diminished in size to become a public footpath adjacent to the southern boundary of the old Hillside Convent, leading through Pinehurst to Cove.

Another street which tells a story is Union Street, formerly called Workhouse Lane. Leading from the turnpike towards Cove, it originally gave access to the Farnborough Workhouse, which was built to provide accommodation and work for the poor.

Following enclosure, the resulting economies in farming methods caused much homelessness in rural areas. In 1782 the Gilbert Act enabled parishes to join together in a union to erect workhouses for such people. In 1793 the parishes of Farnborough, Cove, Hartley Wintney, Hawley and Yateley became incorporated and built a workhouse, on the borders with Cove, on four acres of land given by the lord of the manor. In 1796 the vestry agreed to sell an old almshouse to pay back the money it borrowed for furnishing the workhouse.

The government appointed the Poor Law Commissioners to administer the national system throughout the country and the house was run by a master and matron appointed on an annual contract. The inmates at Farnborough generally grew vegetables, looked after the livestock or carried out household tasks to keep the place clean. Some of the more able men and older boys were sent to work for local farmers. Advertisements appeared regularly in the *Reading Mercury*, the only local newspaper at that time, seeking tenders for the supply of basic foodstuffs such as bread, flour, lard, butter, salt and tea as well as soap and candles. The cheaper cuts of meat such as mutton, brisket and clods of beef were also supplied under contract along with essentials such as shoes and clothing.

In comparison with other workhouses, the inmates at Farnborough seem to have fared well. They had a reasonable diet, sanitary accommodation and work was often found for them. A medical officer was appointed who visited regularly to tend to the sick and latterly to administer vaccinations when these were made obligatory by the government. Elementary schooling was given to the children. However, towards the middle of the 19th century, conditions appear to have deteriorated and many complaints were being recorded. The workhouse closed in 1868 and the occupants were transferred to Hartley Wintney.

The house was put up for sale in 1871 and sold for £400, the money being put towards the newly erected National School. Renamed Wilmot House, the old workhouse was then occupied for some time by Frederick Lunn, a cattle and pig dealer, and eventually sold for demolition in the 1980s.

Responsibility for the poor had been placed on to the individual parishes by various Acts of Parliament. Taxes had to be raised in order to help feed, house and clothe those people who could not support themselves. The administration fell to an overseer who was chosen from among the people of high standing in the parish. He and the churchwardens were

Farnborough Incorporation
Dietary for Adult Paupers

RECEIVED
P.L.B.
APR 20
1853

		Breakfast		Dinner						Supper	
		Bread	Gruel	Cooked Meat	Vegeta-bles	Soup	Bread	Cheese	Rice or Suet Pudding	Bread	Cheese
		oz.	pints.	oz.	oz.	pints.	oz.	oz.	oz.	oz.	oz.
Sunday..	Men..	6	1½	5	16					6	2
	Women	5	1½	5	16					5	1½
Monday..	Men..	6	1½			2	4			6	2
	Women	5	1½			2	4			5	1½
Tuesday..	Men..	6	1½				7	2		6	2½
	Women	5	1½				5	1½		5	1½
Wednesday.	Men..	6	1½	Bacon 5			5			6	2
	Women	5	1½	4			5			5	1½
Thursday..	Men..	6	1½						14	6	2
	Women	5	1½						12	5	1½
Friday..	Men..	6	1½	Bacon 5			5			6	2
	Women	5	1½	4			5			5	1½
Saturday..	Men..	6	1½				7	2		6	2
	Women	5	1½				5	1½		5	1½

Old People of Sixty Years of age and upwards may be allowed One Ounce of Tea, Four Ounces of Butter and seven Ounces of Sugar per Week instead of Cheese and Gruel for Supper and Breakfast if deemed expedient to make this change.

Children under nine Years of Age to be dieted at discretion. above Nine to be allowed the same Quantities as Women.

The Sick to be dieted as directed by the Medical Officer.

17 Diet sheet for adult paupers at the workhouse in 1853.

18 Map of workhouse from Sale Plan of 1871.

MAP OF
FARNBOROUGH UNION WORKHOUSE,
AND LAND ADJOINING,
SITUATE CLOSE TO
FARNBOROUGH STATION,
ON THE S.W. RAILWAY.

Scale 2 Chains to an Inch.

charged with the task of collecting rates and distributing the money according to the needs of the individual families. Applications for additional handouts were considered at the regular meetings conducted in the church vestry. The parish vestry meetings originally took place annually to elect churchwardens, but had gradually become the forum for discussing parish matters not directly involved with the church. The minutes of these meetings in Farnborough survive from 1726 and reveal much about life in the parish at the time.

There are numerous entries showing amounts given out to families in the village who took in orphans or old people. Payments were made to certain people for curing sickness or injury. Occasionally a carpenter would be paid for 'making ye coffin' or 'mending ye church roof or shingles'. An entry in 1730 for 'straw for the Almshouse' helps to establish that, when it was sold in 1796, the almshouse had been in existence for at least 66 years.

Other useful information about life under the lord of the manor can be gleaned from the parish registers. During the reign of Elizabeth I, it was decreed that all parishes should keep records of its christenings, weddings and burials. Initially this rule was not always adhered to very satisfactorily; some parishes could not afford special books and often the parish clerk was a little careless in his record keeping. In 1597 it was further decreed that special parchment register books should be purchased by every parish and all the information held for previous years should be collected and copied into the new books. Farnborough did not conform immediately, but in 1599 a new register was purchased and entries from 1584 were duly copied in a very neat, readable script. Subsequent entries are not always so legible, particularly where the register has been affected by damp or over-exposure to sunlight.

It is interesting to be able to chart the lives of individual families such as that of

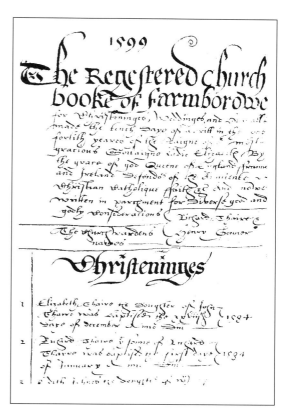

19   The title page of the first parish register for Farnborough.

Edmund, a foundling given the name of Edmund de Farnborough in 1700. His marriage is recorded in 1729 and subsequent baptisms and marriages of his children. He acquired the tenancy of some land which was inherited by his son, Edmund, who is recorded as paying rent for the years 1785 to 1801. It can also be noted from the burial registers that a number of people died of smallpox in the late 1700s. On two occasions, sailors from Gosport died whilst travelling on the coach along the turnpike in Farnborough. Amongst other things, this information is useful corroboration of the destinations of the coaches travelling along the turnpike.

Chapter Three

Turnpikes and Railroads

The very earliest roads were mere tracks used mainly by travellers on foot or on horseback. Over a period of time established routes emerged, but their courses often changed or were diverted when wet weather made passage difficult.

Early descriptions of the physical characteristics of the surrounding area are fairly consistent. They describe the terrain as a vast wasteland prone to sandstorms, interspersed with marshy bogs, and considered one of the most inhospitable areas through which to travel. But travel through it was necessary from around the 14th century when the West Country ports were opening up and becoming commercially important. The best route out of London to the west followed a medieval route through Hounslow and Staines, where it crossed the River Thames to climb up the hill towards Bagshot. At Bagshot the road split, with the main road heading down through Blackwater to Southampton and beyond to Exeter, and the minor routes leading through Frimley and Farnborough down to Portsmouth and Gosport via Farnham and Winchester.

It is noticeable that the road does not, in fact, touch the centre of the villages of Farnborough, Cove or Aldershot but takes a route on slightly higher ground on the outskirts of each. In his book *The Lost Roads of Wessex*, C. Cochrane explains: 'The road deliberately avoided the Saxon villages of Cove, Farnborough and Aldershot, which rather confirms the opinion that its final course followed a trend often found with medieval roads [possibly to preserve the village street] that, unless there were definite posting facilities, the main highway was taken away from the village.' This route also avoided the marshy areas between Farnborough and Cove where, even today, much of the land is very wet. When building has taken place the presence of water has always been a problem.

The Highway Act of 1555 placed the responsibility of road maintenance on to the parishes through which they passed. The manorial records in Farnborough include numerous occasions when inhabitants were put to work on the roads. In December 1836 a man applied to the parish for poor relief and was ordered 'to dig gravel for use on the roads'. That same year tenders were sought from local farmers for 'carting gravel to the roads leading from the turnpike to Coleford Bridge, the crossways in The Street, from the crossways in The Street to *The Ship* and from *The Ship* to Hawley Bridge'. The contract for the road from The Street to *The Ship* was awarded 'to Mr Marsh at 1/9d per cart load'.

However, the main route through the parish, the turnpike, required considerably more upkeep than the local roads because of the increasing volume of commercial through-traffic using it. As this was a problem experienced throughout the country, the government had introduced a system whereby the user was expected to pay for the upkeep of the highway. Turnpike trusts were set up by Acts of Parliament, and they charged tolls or fees to allow travellers to pass. The trusts were ordered to erect milestones along the routes and guide posts at road junctions. The tolls varied according to the size of the wheels on the carts and wagons, and even the drovers with their herds of animals had to pay according to the number of animals passing through. Consequently the drovers would, whenever possible, avoid the turnpikes and take their animals across the commons and byways. George Sturt in his biography, *A Farmer's Life* published in 1922, notes his uncle's memories of the drovers coming in to the Blackwater Fair from the Welsh hills: 'They came never touchin' the turnpike roads. They'd lose a day goin' round sooner'n they'd pass a 'gate'.'

The turnpike through Farnborough was regularly used by the coach from London to Gosport. The *Farnham Almanac* shows in 1837 that 'The Express' arrived in Farnham at 1 o'clock daily having passed through Farnborough earlier in the day. George Sturt's uncle also recalled that, 'The stage coaches stopped at the *Tumbledown Dick* and not the stage coaches only. Road wagons—those cumbersome predecessors of the modern goods train—were wont to call at the 'Tumbledown' on their lumbering journeys to London.'

The turnpike trusts were not profitable and built up large debts. The trustees borrowed against projected receipts which did not materialise, did not use all the money to maintain the roads, and had little control over the individual tollgates. The seven-mile stretch of turnpike between Frimley Bridge and Farnham, traversing Farnborough and Aldershot, came under the jurisdiction of the Winchester Turnpike Trust. It was uneconomical, as evidenced in a letter from Mr. Hollest, the Clerk of the Winchester Turnpike Trust, discussed at the parish vestry meeting in 1865. The parish was asked if it would agree to the dissolution of the Trust. The letter pointed out that if the road ceased to be a turnpike, it would then be the responsibility of the parish to repair it. The parish refused the request, saying that abolition of the Trust would 'inflict upon this Parish an unjust

20   Frimley Bridge carried the turnpike road across the parish and county boundary.

and grievous injury by throwing upon it (already charged to the District Highway Board with a very heavy rate for the repair of the highways) the additional burden of repairing exclusively a distance of three miles and upwards of the turnpike road used for the purposes of the heavy traffic to and from Aldershott Camp'.

The census in 1861 shows that Frederick Withall was the toll collector, and in 1871 it was George Reeves. Both censuses indicate the toll cottage as being south of the *Tumbledown Dick*, and the turnpike gate is clearly marked on the 1871 Ordnance Survey map. There is still a milestone nearby indicating 32 miles from London, 5 from Bagshot and 8 to Farnham. There was another tollgate just outside the parish, beside the *Row Barge Inn* on the Farnham side of the Basingstoke Canal. When the *Row Barge Inn* was demolished, the tollgate appears

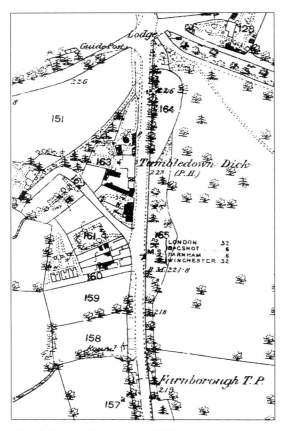

21 Ordnance Survey map of 1871, showing Turnpike Gate, milestone and guide post.

22 Ordnance Survey map of 1856, showing Bridge Gate Toll Bar.

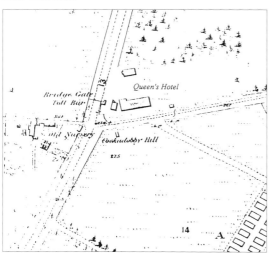

to have been moved northwards into Farnborough, as it is shown on an 1856 Ordnance Survey map as the Bridge Gate Toll Bar immediately adjacent to the *Queen's Hotel*. Milestone number 33 can still be seen almost opposite the *Swan Inn*.

Responsibility for the main highways was eventually transferred from the Turnpike Trust in the early 1870s to the Hartley Wintney Highways District, who acted for the County Council. An advertisement in *Sheldrake's Military Gazette* in 1874 refers to the contract for repairing the late turnpike road, indicating a recent transference of responsibility.

Increasing Army Camp traffic was also causing problems along the edge of the North Camp at Lynchford Road, which by 1856 was already opening up to new shops and houses. This old carriage road was developing into a regular thoroughfare and required much gravel to keep it in repair. Amos Yates, a forage contractor and one of the first traders in Lynchford Road, was authorised to carry out the work but the burden on the parish rate was considerable. The South Eastern Railway, constructed along the eastern boundary of the village, required easier access to the North Camp from its new station at Lynchford, now called North Camp. This entailed building a bridge across the river where previously there had been a ford. As the river was the parish boundary, permission was sought from both Farnborough and Ash parish councils and the bridge was constructed about 1858.

One of the regular users of the turnpike was the Royal Mail coach. The Royal Mail archives reveal that in 1813 a survey of the South of England was undertaken by their surveyor, a Mr. Scott. Farnborough is shown on the mail coach route which ran through Hounslow, Staines, Bagshot, Frimley, Farnborough, Farnham, and Winchester to the South Coast. The Farnborough Receiving House is shown at the end of a walk from Bagshot, Blackwater and Hawley. Mr Scott's map indicates that the mail was taken on foot from Bagshot, via those villages

23 Bridge over the River Blackwater at North Camp railway station in 1960, when fleets of Aldershot & District buses took visitors to the airshow.

along the Hawley Lane, which was on a slightly more northern route than today, and delivered to *The Ship*.

The *Post Office Trades Directory* of 1847 shows Thomas Elstone at *The Ship* inn and Post Office, with letters being received through the Bagshot office. This system was still in operation in 1852 when a letter was sent by the rector of Farnborough from his address at Farnborough Rectory, Bagshot. Later that year, the Royal Mail began to use the new railway system more extensively, and by the end of 1852 they were paying rent to the London and South Western Railway for using rooms at Farnborough Station.

The London and Southampton Railway Company had come into existence in 1832. In 1834 a Bill was put before Parliament and work commenced on the first section of line from Nine Elms to Woking. The proposed line through Farnborough went across the Glebe Fields between the Old Rectory and Highgate Lane and did not meet with total accord among the villagers. The parish vestry committee considered a proposal by the railway company to compensate the parish for allowing the railway to cross a pathway in regular use between the village and the church. In order not to create a barrier between the old village and the church, the vestry committee requested the company to construct a cartway over their railroad, as they called it then, to link up with Highgate Lane. Today, Church Path still carries a footbridge over the railway at that same point.

Progress was slow and it was not until 1838 that the line opened up through Farnborough to Winchfield, and thence to Basingstoke by 1839. The line was being laid northwards from Southampton and had reached Winchester by this time but the journey between Basingstoke and Winchester still necessitated coach travel.

At last, in May 1840, the whole of the line was opened to both commercial and passenger traffic, but this was no transport of comfort. Initially passenger traffic was affordable only by the rich, and was seasonal, particularly during the summer months when the first 'cheap day' excursions were run. The coaches were lightweight and built on a similar design to stage-coaches, affording little protection to travellers being buffeted around at 20 miles per hour. First-class passengers travelled inside the carriages sitting three abreast on seats facing each other with so little space their knees touched. Second-class carriages had wooden benches and open sides, with no more room and hardly any weather protection. The poor were not catered for at all until the whole line was opened and third-class travel was made available. Even then, these unfortunate passengers had to travel in open trucks normally used for livestock, but converted by the insertion of crude basket-type seating.

The guard, who controlled the brake, fared little better than a third-class passenger. He sat in a seat on the roof of the first-class carriage. His only protection against the elements was his smart uniform of tunic and trousers made of a sturdy material complete with silver buttons and a lace collar; not very protective on a wet and windy journey across the wild heathlands of Hampshire!

Early steam engines were not very powerful and often the trains could not manage the inclines, particularly with a heavy load. Sometimes two engines were used and frequently couplings broke under the strain leaving carriages stranded. Early signalling was by flags and the impending arrival or departure was indicated by the ringing of a handbell. Local policemen were called off their beats to patrol the railway lines, also acting as ticket collectors and signalmen. A train would only leave the station if the preceding one was no longer in sight. This rather casual approach gave rise to numerous accidents. These accidents obviously caused great public concern about the safety of this new-fangled transport and incidents were reported in *The Times* with monotonous regularity.

In June 1840 an engine collided with a train at Farnborough injuring a number of passengers and damaging the two rear horse carriages. An enraged passenger wrote to *The Times* berating the carelessness which had caused the accident and the indifference shown by the railway company towards the high incidence of such disasters. A fatality did occur in 1859 when, according to *The Times*, 'shunting carriages passing over one of the Company's servants, severed his head from his body'. The deceased was a Mr. Harwood whose remains were taken to the *New Inn* for the inquest where the coroner recorded a verdict of accidental death.

After the connection to Gosport was made in 1841, Farnborough Station became very important as a destination for royalty *en route* to Windsor from the naval dockyards. This was probably the reason that such an imposing station, designed by architect William Twite, was built similar in design, although smaller, to the one at Gosport.

Contemporary accounts of Queen Victoria's arrival at Farnborough in 1844 paint a vivid picture at a time when engravings were the only way of illustrating the news. This was probably Her Majesty's first visit to Farnborough. Having travelled by road from Windsor, the royal party arrived at the station entrance where, according to the *Illustrated London News*, a 'sumptuous red carpet had been laid down'. Inside there were reception rooms for royal use. The main reception room, which cost £130 to construct, had 'gold filigree work on the ceiling, with a grand marble chimneypiece surrounding the fireplace and very expensive furnishings as befitted this early Royal station'. Subsequently these fittings, together with the fireplace, were removed to the new royal station at Windsor when it opened in 1851.

24   The staff at Farnborough (L&SW) Station in the 1880s. The station was subsequently rebuilt.

25   King Louis Philippe of France arriving at Farnborough *en route* to Windsor from Gosport in 1844. The signal, towering above the station, was a disc rotated by a rope indicating, according to the position of the aperture, which lines were blocked or clear. The station sign indicates that Farnborough is the nearest station to Camberley, Sandhurst and Bagshot.

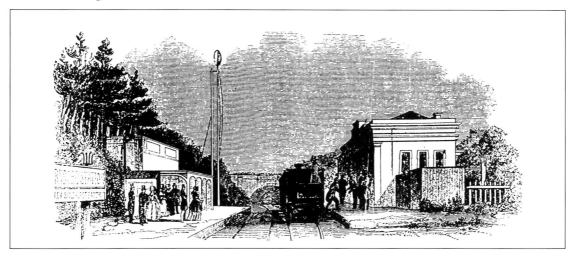

The royal railway carriages, according to the *Illustrated London News*, were equally lavish:

> The ceilings are of white damask embroidered with crimson and adorned by national emblems and crowns. The draperies are of crimson and white figured satin damask richly lined and trimmed; the blinds are of peach blossom silk with crimson silk and silver tassels. Some ingenious lamps enable the royal passengers to see at night and when passing through tunnels. The whole richly carpeted in Axminster over a patent composition of cork and rubber to prevent the unpleasant vibration incident to railway travelling ... externally the carriages were of dark maroon with royal arms emblazoned across them; the door handles were solid silver and the windows were of superb embossed and ground glass.

Soon after the upheaval of the construction of the South Western line, another railway was built through Farnborough which followed the course of the River Blackwater. With other railway companies opening up more lines, the intention was to link the Channel ports with the north and west without having to go through London. It was felt there would be great opportunities for farmers to widen their markets, hop growers in the west could obtain their hop poles from Kent and Sussex more economically, and the magistrates and court judiciary would be able to travel more easily between the county towns of Guildford and Reading. As supporting evidence of the need for the new line, traffic censuses were taken at the various intended stations on the route, including Farnborough. All travellers through the village were asked to give details about their destinations and reasons for travel.

In the original Bill put before Parliament in 1846, there were plans to link up with the London & Southampton Railway by building spurs from both the Reading and Guildford directions. By 1847 the contracts for the works from Reading to Farnborough had been let to a Mr. Jackson but progress at the Farnborough end was slow because of indecision about the spurs. The only spur that materialised was the one from the Reading direction eastwards towards London; there was no direct connection from Guildford westwards towards Basingstoke.

When the whole line opened in 1849, Farnborough had a temporary wooden station pending the decision on a permanent connection with the London & Southampton Railway. The London & Southampton agreed that the new railway could run its trains to the Frimley junction for passengers to change trains but the expenses of signalling, building a station and stopping the trains would have to be borne by the Reading Guildford & Reigate Railway. The station at Frimley junction was never built, although a few trains were run on to the London line, because it was not cost effective.

Abandoning the second spur saved money but incurred compensation costs. Mr. Morant, the chief landowner affected, claimed that his surveyor had unnecessarily agreed all the sale arrangements which were then dropped. The contract for the construction of the Guildford line from Farnborough to Ash was let to Mr. Furness and was an easier section to construct, although a cutting was necessary to take the new railway under the London line.

The railways initially had a limited effect on the local economy. There was, of course, a new form of employment and the records show quite a number of railway related occupations being undertaken. Some local labour had been employed during the construction and outside labourers needed lodging rooms. The *New Inn* was built just outside the London South Western station and was used as a posting house

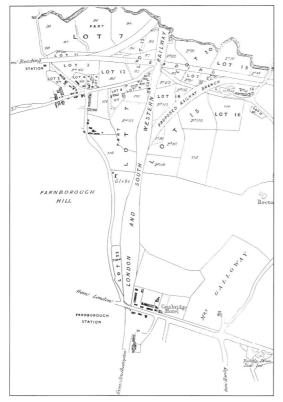

26 Extract from map of auction lots in a sale of 1860, which shows the site of a proposed spur to link rail traffic from Guildford to the Southampton line.

27   The *Railway Hotel*, formerly the *New Inn*, now known as the *Ham and Blackbird*, in 1902. In the centre is the bridge over the railway, with the post office, Jubilee Hall and *The Cambridge Hotel* on the right.

to receive the mail until a post room was opened in the station itself.

The year 1854 saw the arrival of the army in nearby Aldershot, but until 1870 the town had no railway station, so large numbers of the military came through Farnborough. It was a common sight to see a body of two or three hundred men in their colourful tunics marching along the Farnborough Road to and from the Camp. The *Illustrated London News* in October 1855 commented on one such group numbering 310 soldiers from the Grenadier Guards who departed by train from Farnborough to South-ampton *en route* to the Crimea. The same report noted that the area surrounding the station was still very tranquil, isolated from the old village and surrounded by trees where the song of the nightingale was frequently heard.

The following year, between April and October, over 95,000 troops passed through the station. On occasions they marched up to 500 at a time and caused utter confusion when they turned up at the wrong station. Now-adays the station on the South Eastern line is called Farnborough North, but for many years both were known as Farnborough.

A vivid picture is painted by a daily diary kept by Joseph Denner Blake, who came to Farnborough as the telegraph operator for The Electric & International Telegraph Company. Arriving from Basingstoke in November 1855, he found his working conditions at the L & SW railway station to be very 'draughty, cold and cramped'. The facilities for royalty and visitors may have been quite grand but conditions for the staff obviously needed improvement. There being no lodging houses nearby, he had to walk into the old village where he found a room with the station master of the South Eastern Railway. When he took messages to the Army Camp at Aldershot he thought it was 'a wild looking place, with huts stuck up on the open common'. He discovered that there was a picket with an armed guard on sentry duty on the road between the *New Inn* and the *Tumbledown Dick*. No soldier from the Camp was allowed to pass towards the station without producing a ticket or a permit.

As the volume of rail and military traffic increased, Farnborough rapidly expanded to

To H.R.H. The Duke of Connaught and H.I.M. The Empress Eugénie.

Telephone No. 36.

Established 50 Years.

JOYCE Brothers Coach Builders & Motor Engineers & Body Builders

District Agents for the New Valveless Cars. Agents for all the best Makes of Cars including Sunbeams & Swifts. Carriages Warehoused. Let on hire and Sold on Commission. Stockists of Dunlop, Michelin, Hutchinson & Self Sealing Company's Tyres & Tubes. Any other make supplied. Retreaded or Repaired. Vacuum & Price's Oils & Grease in Stock. Pratt's Shell and Carburine Motor Spirit. Special Quotations for Quantities. Cars Repaired, painted and Upholstered a Speciality. Certificated Repairers to The Motor Union and other Insurance Companies. Gears, Magnetos & Electric Work Fitted and every requisite required for Motors supplied. Bodies Built to Customers' own Designs and Chassis.

Farnborough Station, Hants.

28 A page from a *Guide* to Farnborough in 1907. The Joyce brothers adapted their former wheelwright business to accommodate the motor car. These premises were on the Farnborough Road, near the *Tumbledown Dick*, considered in those days to be near the station.

meet its needs. The *Duke of Cambridge Hotel* was built opposite the *New Inn* along with a number of shops and business premises. Mr. A. Hitchcock had premises at Farnborough Station as an egg and fruit importer. A farrier and saddler, a wheelwright, a brewery agent and a coal merchant all set up in the station yard, which soon became overcrowded. By April 1857 the railway company had purchased all the land from the workhouse up to the *New Inn* and had greatly enlarged the station premises. Some of the traders then moved on to the Farnborough Road.

In 1855, when Mr. George Carter was station master, his daughter Charlotte was the postmistress. By this time the mail was coming in by train. Letters arrived at the office at 7 a.m. and 11 a.m. each day and outgoing post was despatched at 9.30 p.m. and 10.20 a.m. Within a very short time, thanks to the rapid increase in the volume of mail for the Camp, the railway company had to relocate the post office in larger premises in the station yard. Mr. Dean then took over as postmaster and Mr. Carter became innkeeper at the *Tumbledown Dick*.

Joseph Blake's diaries show that telegraph messages for the camp were increasing and often necessitated a trip in the dogcart which he hired from Mr. Carter. The charge for such deliveries was 6d. a mile; that was over and above the cost of sending the message which varied from 1s. 6d. for 20 words to London to 5s. to Dublin. Messages could also be sent to Europe. The diary records that 1,002 messages passed through the telegraph office during August 1856. On some days he was so busy he did not have time to eat his lunch, only to snatch a biscuit.

People began to collect their mail from the new post office although some special deliveries were made to the big houses such as The Grange, Farnborough Hill and The Manor House. By 1860 letters were also being delivered to the old post office in Farnborough village as well as the sub-post offices near the *Queen's Hotel* and in Lynchford Road. When a pillar box was installed at the station, letters were no longer handed in over the counter. During the summer months additional sorters had to be employed to cope with the huge number of letters for the soldiers encamped on Farnborough Common for their summer drills.

All the inns nearby and even those a mile or so away in the old village capitalised on the increased rail traffic and would send a coach or 'fly' to meet the trains. A fly was not much more than a cart with seats but it was transport of a kind and obviously much needed, judging by the number of cab and fly proprietors listed in the directories of the day. A horse-drawn omnibus service to Aldershot run by Mr. J. Barwick, who lived next door to the *Duke of Cambridge Hotel*, was well established by 1859. Tilbury of Aldershot also ran an omnibus which, according to the adverts, 'left the coach station at South Camp half an hour before every up train from Farnborough, passing the *Queen's Hotel* North Camp a quarter of an hour after leaving the coach office'.

In 1861 discussions and public meetings took place in Aldershot to consider yet another revolutionary form of transport, a horse-drawn tram or omnibus on rails. This purported to be more comfortable than either being thrown around in a train or jolted along a road full of potholes. The idea was eagerly adopted, and The Aldershot Street Rail Company was formed. However, despite numerous revisions of plans, the dissolution of the company and a new company being formed, no construction work took place until 1878, when the Aldershot & Farnborough Tramways Company was authorised by Act of Parliament to undertake the project. The tramshed was built on a triangular piece of land on the south side of Workhouse Lane, near the *Railway Hotel*. The line was laid on the west side of Farnborough Road, past the *Tumbledown Dick*, up Star Hill, along the common, and past the *Swan Inn* until it reached the *Queen's Hotel*, where it turned left along the south side of Lynchford Road, terminating at North Camp Station.

LONDON & SOUTH WESTERN RAILWAY.

NOTICE.

ON

HER MAJESTY'S VISIT

TO

SANDHURST,

On **MONDAY, 2nd of JUNE,**

OMNIBUSES

Will be in attendance at

FARNBOROUGH STATION,

To convey Passengers, on the arrival of the Up and Down Morning Trains, viz., the 9 a.m. from Southampton, and 7.15 a.m. from London.

FARE, there & back, 7s.

As the number of Omnibuses is limited, Tickets to secure places can be obtained (not later than 12 o'clock on the previous day) at the following Stations :—Waterloo, Kingston, Farnboro,' Andover, Winchester, Bishopstoke, Southampton and Portsmouth

29 Poster advertising details of the omnibuses which would transport passengers to Sandhurst during Queen Victoria's visit in 1856.

A tremendous amount of effort was put into the planning of the tramway over a period of forty years, yet very little physical evidence of its existence survives. A detailed study in *The Tramway Review* in 1963 reveals that the Board of Trade issued a Certificate of Safety in 1881 although there is no record of an official opening. In 1883 the returns to the Board of Trade record receipts from passengers amounting to £246. Bearing in mind that the workman's fare before 6 a.m. was advertised at 1s. 2d. a journey, and that in that same year 24,600 passengers travelled, the cost per mile was probably about 2d. At that price, with running costs of £865, it is little wonder the enterprise did not appear to last long, as indicated by the fact there were no Board of Trade returns after 1884. However, in 1889 *Kelly's Directory* lists the Tramway Manager as being Frank Spicer, and the 1891 census corroborates this. According to the recollections of local inhabitants in the 1960s, the tramway still had limited use until the early 1900s. It is also recorded that, when the foundation stone of the new Town Hall was laid in 1896, Mr. Dever, the first Chairman of the new Urban District Council, hired a tramcar to take the official guests from the station to the site of the new building. Over subsequent years pieces of tramway appeared as various roadworks were undertaken but the only photographic evidence is the occasional postcard showing some of the exposed tracks along the route.

The last attempt at reviving the old tramway schemes was in 1896 but again it failed, possibly because of the new Light Railways Act which opened the way for other ambitious ideas to electrify the transport system between Farnborough and Aldershot. These too failed, although some additional track was laid along the Farnborough Road only to be removed at the request of the Council who complained of the danger that some of the exposed parts of the line were causing to the newest innovation, motorised vehicles!

The first motor bus ran from Aldershot to Farnborough South Western Railway Station on 1 June 1906. It was an experimental run, with the passengers being drawn from civic dignitaries. It took 17½ minutes to complete the route along the Queen's Avenue, via Farnborough Town Hall. The press reports state

30   Tramtracks (in the bottom left-hand corner of the picture) on Lynchford Road in 1905.

31   Aldershot & District Traction Company buses on an outing in the 1920s.

that the journey time could have been shorter if it had not been for 'the considerable detours to pass a portion of the road up for repairs'— nothing changes.

A company called the Aldershot & Farnborough Motor Omnibus Co. Ltd. was registered but operational difficulties soon dogged it. The company was bought out in 1912 by the British Electric Traction Company Ltd., who went on to form the Aldershot & District Traction Company Ltd. This company, fondly nicknamed 'The Tracco' or on occasions 'Ave a shot and risk it', was the basis of the public transport system between the two towns to the present day, although its name disappeared when the company was acquired by Stagecoach.

Chapter Four

Economic Growth

The arrival of the army in Aldershot, and the establishment of the North Camp at the southern end of Farnborough, opened up attractive opportunities for investors. In the early 1860s the large expanse of heathland to the south of the Farnborough Park Estate was sold for residential development. Two property companies were formed with the aim of purchasing, building on and then leasing numerous plots to growing numbers of military officers arriving in the area. The Farnborough and Aldershot Freehold and Ground Rent Society Ltd. was incorporated in 1862 and, although its name was associated with a large number of properties, the company was dissolved in 1882. A more active organisation, The Farnborough Cottage Company, was formed in 1863 and became a limited company in 1864. The share capital was £20,000 divided into 400 shares of £50 each. Three of the shareholders were Edward Chatfield, Henry Curry and William Knell, all of whom had a profound influence on the growth of south Farn-borough.

Edward Chatfield, acting as the agent for the company, came to Farnborough in 1863, accompanied by Henry Curry, an architect. Together they planned the layout of the area stretching south from Sycamore Road, formerly designated as the New Park on the Manor Estate. The attractive layout and symmetrical design of the wide, tree-lined roads is attrib-uted to Mr. Curry, who had previously been working in the new coastal resort of Eastbourne and brought his ideas from there. He took

lodgings at the nearby *Swan* inn on the Farnborough Road.

Much of the road building was under-taken by military engineers but the road names were decided upon by Mr. Chatfield, who wanted to reflect people or events connected with the town. The primary road leading to the Camp was Alexandra Road, named after Alexandra Princess of Wales, wife of the future King Edward VII, who rode along it on a visit to the North Camp. Church Circle and Church Road denote that, from the outset, the devel-opers envisaged that a new church would be required. In the event the church was built on a different site.

The first houses to be built were Stirling Villas, on Alexandra Road, one of which became the home of Mr. Chatfield. These three pairs of three-storey semi-detached villas are still standing, albeit with considerable altera-tions. Blackwell House, almost opposite, soon followed, as did a number of similarly styled large, double-fronted villas such as Pierremont, now demolished, in Cambridge Road. At the other end of the road, near the Camp, Alpha Villas, a set of six slightly smaller, semi-detached dwellings, were erected by another developer, Mr. Thick, and the scene was set for expansion over the next forty years.

Mr. Chatfield went on to build Croxted House, on the corner of Alexandra and Boundary Road, in about 1865. Initially let to Capt. Martin John Wheatley of the Royal Engineers, it subsequently became a school in the ownership of the Cumberbatch family,

32 *The Swan* inn, *c*.1903, where Mr. Curry stayed when planning the layout of the roads in South Farnborough.

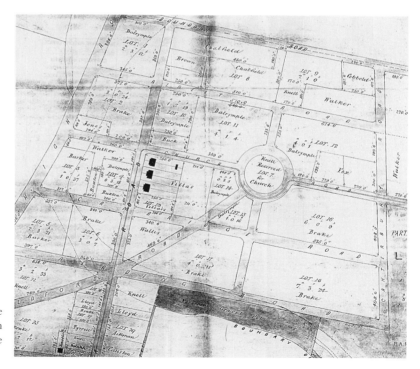

33 Extract from plan of sale of the Knellwood Estate in 1875, showing the layout of the roads in South Farnborough.

34   Pierremont House, Cambridge Road.

35   Crossways, Alexandra Road, formerly Croxted House.

CROSSWAYS SCHOOL

FARNBOROUGH

For Sons and Daughters of Officers and Professional Men only

RUN ON P.N.E.U. LINES
INCLUDING
Music, French, Latin, Drill, Games, Dancing, Fencing

Aldershot, Farnborough and Cove Buses pass the door

For Prospectus apply:

(Principal) Miss VIOLET K. SKRIMSHIRE,
"Crossways," Alexandra Road, Farnborough

A limited number of Boarders received.   Entire charge of children whose parents are abroad.

36 An advertisement for Crossways School in 1929.

followed by the Misses Skrimshire in the 1920s. The Farnborough Library had its home there for many years and it is now used as offices for a travel company.

Another early entrepreneur and shareholder in the Farnborough Cottage Company Ltd. who found Farnborough attractive was Mr. William Knell, a businessman who had made his fortune in cotton.

Deeds and documents from 1861 show him purchasing land in his own right as well as on behalf of the company. The land on which the College of Technology now stands was the site of three of Mr. Knell's houses, all built in the 1860s. The most impressive was Castleden Hall, an imposing double-fronted three-storey building standing in nine acres of land, which he occupied in 1867. The house was set well back from the Farnborough Road and the plans show beautifully designed formal gardens.

In 1871 the occupant was John Swindell, a city merchant, and in 1873 Castleden Hall was sold to the Rev. Arthur Henry Alwyn Morton MA. He greatly enlarged it and ran it as Farnborough School for the sons of officers and gentlemen. Sport was considered an important part of their education, so playing fields were acquired across the Farnborough Road and accessed by a tunnel built beneath it. One of the first cricket matches played by the school was against the Farnborough Choir in Rectory Meadows on 28 July 1873. Football

37 William Knell, an influential developer who came to Farnborough in the early 1860s and built a number of large houses over a twenty-year period.

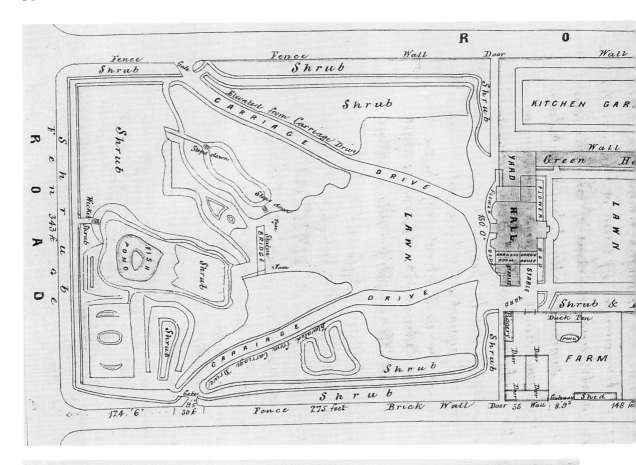

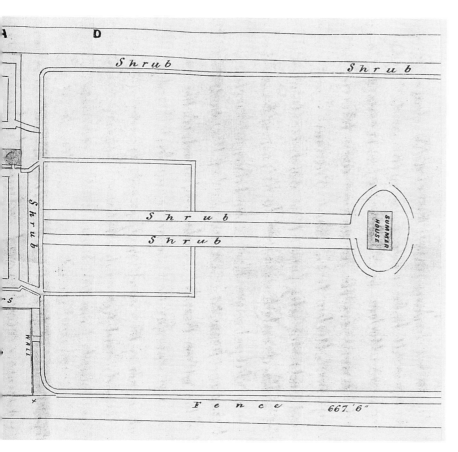

A   D

Shrub   *Shrub*

Shrub

Shrub   *Shrub*

Shrub

SUMMER HOUSE

WALL

Fence   667' 6"

38   An extract from the deeds of Castleden Hall on the corner of Farnborough Road and Boundary Road. A formal front garden was a status symbol in Victorian society and was particularly pertinent for Castleden Hall, as it was on the route taken by visiting royalty on their way to inspect the troops in Aldershot. The road on the left is Farnborough Road.

39   Letter addressed to Farnborough School. The postmark on the reverse reads, 'Farnborough Station FB 12 78'.

was also very prominent. A letter to Victor Middleton, a 12-year-old pupil in 1878, from his older brother Alf, asks whether he is 'distinguishing himself at football and winning all his games'. Victor, like many of the boys at the school, went on to finish his education at Eton.

Following demolition of the old buildings, the Farnborough College of Technology was erected on the site in the 1950s. A few trees from an avenue of firs have survived and been incorporated into the landscaping of one of the walkways of this modern place of learning.

Two large semi-detached villas called Mapperton Lodge and Park Lodge were built on land adjoining Castleden Hall at the junction of Sycamore Road and Farnborough Road. The two were altered to become Park House, which was occupied by Mr. Knell in 1878. In the

early 1920s this became Belgrave House School, which catered for boys of seven to 15 years and prepared them for public schools and the Royal Naval College at Dartmouth. This school, too, was subsequently demolished to make way for the College.

The best known of Mr. Knell's houses, and the only place where his memory is perpetuated, is Knellwood, which today is a residential home for elderly people. Sometimes referred to as Knellwood Hall, it was possibly the first house that Mr. Knell built in Farnborough. His name first appears on the deeds when the land was conveyed to him in 1861. By the 1871 census, the house had been built and was occupied by Robert William Staff, a captain in the Royal Engineers, although Mr. Knell himself was then living in The Sycamores. Then followed occupation by Sir Thomas

40   Farnborough School grounds, *c*.1900. A few trees from this avenue survive in the landscaping of the College of Technology today.

41   Belgrave House School in the 1920s. The enlarged house was originally two villas called Park Lodge and Mapperton Lodge.

42 Knellwood in the 1950s. It has since lost its chimneys and been greatly extended but the elderly residents of this home can still enjoy the lovely surroundings of one of the few remaining houses built by William Knell.

Steele, who was General Officer Commanding at Aldershot 1875-80.

The Knellwood Estate stretched from Canterbury Road, eastwards over Sycamore Lane as it then was, across the Reading, Guildford and Reigate Railway, to the Blackwater River. The property was purchased in 1880 by Col. Richard Harrison, of the Royal Engineers, who soon took an active part in local affairs by being on the building committee of the new church of St Mark. A panel of stained glass depicting the Harrison coat of arms has remained in Knellwood and is displayed in a window of the entrance porch.

The beautiful grounds sweeping down Sycamore Hill, as it was known in earlier times, towards Sycamore Lane, hosted numerous fêtes and fairs. Today we know it as King George V playing fields, a very popular public park. At the lower end of the playing fields, near the road, there is an avenue of oak trees which looks as if it might have been a driveway of some sort. Reference to earlier maps shows that this was the original Sycamore Lane which gave access to the old Sycamore Farm.

On the high ground to the north of Sycamore Lane was The Sycamores, a rambling old building, very similar in style to Knellwood, with good views across the Blackwater Valley towards Mytchett. Sir Thomas Westrop McMahon, a former commandant of the

Cavalry Brigade, purchased it early in the 1870s and then sold it in 1884 to Sir Reginald Gipps, secretary to the Duke of Cambridge. In the grounds was an ice house, one of the few known to have been constructed in the parish.

In 1915 the Sycamores was purchased by the nuns from Hillside Convent to take the pupils from Hillside and the nearby St Mary's Day School. The move had been brought about after the War Office had commandeered their old premises for the duration of the First World War. After the war the nuns were able to return the school to the old buildings on the Farnborough Road and The Sycamores was kept as a residence for the boarders and nuns. When the nuns had acquired Farnborough Hill in 1928, The Sycamores returned to private hands. It was then purchased by the Hilder family. Eventually demolished to make way for development, The Sycamores is remembered today by a small cul-de-sac just off Hilder Gardens on the site of the old house.

Hillside Convent was originally a small villa surrounded by pinewoods. Built at right angles to the western side of Farnborough Road, opposite the junction with Sycamore Road, it was purchased by the nuns in 1889. They added a central wing and a chapel at the northern end, both designed by an architect called Hansom whose family is also credited with the design of the Hansom cab. After the

43   The Sycamores in 1928.

44   Hillside Convent grounds, showing the extensive lawns where the pupils used to play hockey and tennis.

First World War, it was later purchased by the Royal Aircraft Establishment in 1945 for use as a technical college. Hillside survives today as offices, but the original part of the house has been demolished to make way for a modern extension.

There is no evidence to indicate that Hillside was one of Mr. Knell's houses, but behind it was another large house, called Forest Lodge, where he lived in 1880. The site now accommodates the offices of Rushmoor Borough Council but the sale particulars in 1924 indicate this was a substantial building which had been in a military family for nearly forty years. People who remember the house recall the large stained glass window over the staircase, similar to the one in Bifrons, another of Mr. Knell's houses.

In the 1881 census Mr. Knell is found living at 'Mr Knell's new house' in Sycamore Road, which can be identified as Bifrons. *Kelly's Directory* of 1885 substantiates this by listing

Mr. Knell living at 'The Bifron'. The house today has been converted into apartments and stands within an associated development having access from Boundary Road.

Pinewood, in Albert Road, was one of Mr. Knell's earlier houses and bore a strong resemblance to Knellwood and Belgrave House. Purchased by the Rev. Frederick Fabian Brackenbury in about 1884, it was run as a preparatory school for sons of gentlemen. Mrs. Brackenbury taught music at the school and former pupils include the composer and song writer of the 1920s, Roger Quilter. The school survived until 1938, when the threat of war brought closure and transfer to Dorset. The building was requisitioned by the War Department for hostel accommodation, and after the war was purchased by Brand Removals and used as a storage depot. The once beautifully landscaped gardens, where a chapel and swimming pool had been constructed for the school, eventually became totally overgrown and one more of Mr. Knell's legacies succumbed to demolition.

Another developer on the south Farnborough scene was Henry Jesty Brake. Born in Closeworth, Somerset, he was an auctioneer who set up in business in Aldershot in 1856. He moved to Farnborough in 1870, bought over 150 acres of land around North Camp and built elegant houses primarily for letting to officers. A number of these are at the southern end of Alexandra Road and in nearby Netley Street, Southampton Street and Osborne Road. Fortunately this stage of the town's growth has been preserved within what is now designated a Conservation Area.

An outward sign of the increasing prosperity of the town came with the construction of the Town Hall. At the end of the 19th century local government was undergoing major change, and in 1894 residents elected a parish council of 12 members from within their midst. The following year the council took on urban status, which was followed by the formation of Farnborough Urban District Council.

The elected members held their first meeting in Mr. Brake's Auction Rooms in January 1896 and, after the business of electing the chairman and officers, urgent discussion ensued on the necessity of a permanent meeting place. The members who had served on the old parish council were mindful of previous meetings held in cramped locations such as the *Tumbledown Dick*, Mr. Brake's rooms or, on one occasion, at the National School in Farnborough Village. This latter venue was very unpopular because the councillors found it difficult to compete with frequent bouts of hymn singing emanating from the meetings of the Band of Hope held in an adjacent room.

Deciding on a suitable location was difficult because each end of the parish had virtually separate communities with an area of superior residences in between. There was no

45   Bifrons in the 1960s.

46 Mr. Brake's Auction Rooms, Lynchford Road, in the 1920s. The first meetings of Farnborough Urban District Council took place here in 1896.

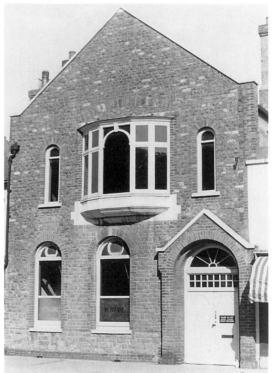

47 Mr. Brake's original premises were destroyed by fire in 1932 and rebuilt the following year. It became an art gallery for a while and is now part of a motorcycle retail outlet.

specific commercial sector, although the area on the Farnborough side of Lynchford Road, on the edge of North Camp, was beginning to develop in a big way. They eventually chose a site at the crossroads where Reading and Guildford Roads intersected with Alexandra Road. This was almost opposite the new church of St Mark and, although some distance from any other commercial activity, it was in the centre of a rising residential area and considered to be the new heart of the town.

The foundation stone was laid on 11 November 1896 amidst a ceremony of military proportions. The *Aldershot News* reported,

> The site was gay with bunting; a large platform, with seating accommodation for some hundreds of people, was provided. The massive foundation stone was suspended by a pulley, and a slanting approach had been made to it, the space being shut off by scaffold poles draped with crimson cloth. In this space there assembled nearly the whole of the members and officials of the District Council, the Architect (Mr George Sherrin), the Builder (Mr Hughes), Mr E Chatfield, whose eighty one summers sit so lightly on him, and Mrs Chatfield, Mrs Brake, Mrs Ewen, and others. Mr & Mrs Dever (the Chairman of the Council and his wife) were cheered when they arrived on the scene. Behind the stone, representatives of the Farnborough Masonic Lodge, and of the Oddfellows, Foresters, and Buffaloes, all wearing the regalia of their Orders, lent colour to the scene. The massed surpliced choirs from the Parish Church and St Mark's with the Rector and Rural Dean (the Rev. A E Kinch), the Vicar of St. Mark's (The Rev. C York Mitchinson) at their head, were grouped at the right of the enclosed space. The spectators who assembled to witness the ceremony must have numbered 1,500 and included many old residents and military persons.

A short dedication service preceded the ceremony performed by Mrs. Dever, who was

48 The Town Hall, *c*.1902.

handed a special silver trowel for the task. Beneath the foundation stone were laid current coins of the realm and copies of *The Times* and the local newspaper, the *Aldershot News*.

Many of the early councillors were businessmen who had been attracted to Farnborough by the development potential of this rising town. It was a comfortable distance from London and no longer considered an isolated and barren wasteland. In fact, it was now quite the reverse and the guide books and directories of the day extolled the virtues of a healthy climate among the numerous pine trees in the vicinity.

The first chairman was Mr. Henry Dever, an accountant who started work with W.W. Deloitte, one of the first public accountants in London. After becoming a partner in the firm of Deloitte, Dever, Griffiths and Co., he settled in Farnborough where he built Farnborough Court and a number of other houses including The Ridges near the Clockhouse on the Farnborough Road.

One of the ongoing problems of a fast developing town was how to deal with the sewage. In the days before buildings were connected to a mains sewage system, contractors

49 The Clockhouse and The Ridges, *c.*1902. The Clockhouse cupola was lowered many years ago when the columns became weak.

50 Bust of Henry Dever, first Chairman of the Council.

51   The Sycamore Road Sewage Works in 1925 following some much needed improvements.

would go round with their carts, often at night time, to collect the sewage waste from private homes. It was then taken to a sewage farm near North Camp station, but until a proper filter system was installed conditions at the farm were very unpleasant.

The sewage from the Army Camp in the early days was a major issue which on one occasion caused the commanding officer of the Camp to be summoned to a vestry meeting. He was requested to make improvements to the camp system as it was seeping sewage into the Blackwater River and causing pollution as the river flowed northwards beside the old village. New army sewage works were constructed at the edge of the camp but the transporting of sewage in open carts from the latrines in North Camp still continued, causing considerable offence for many years.

In 1895 the Council purchased a piece of land from the Knellwood Estate, at the lower

end of Sycamore Road, near the railway. There they constructed a new sewage works for the town. Gradually most of the roads in the town were connected to mains drainage, which necessitated continual upgrading of the system to cope with the additional load. More land was purchased in 1925 and new filtration units were built which considerably eased the situation. Present-day sewage is pumped else-where for treatment so, having served its purpose for nearly one hundred years, the old sewage farm was sold in the 1990s to make way for the development of Sycamore Park.

The water supply to the area has always been good. In the early days wells provided the water but by 1902 three-quarters of all the houses in the district received their supply from the Frimley & Farnborough Water Company at Frimley Green. The remaining wells were inspected regularly by the Council until all houses were connected. It is believed that the last well in regular use was in a domestic garden in Peabody Road and was covered over in 1963. At the time, the user insisted that the well water 'still made the best cuppa in the world'.

Although most of the economic boom of the late 19th century focused on the southern part of the town, the northern end was also seeing significant changes. Farnborough Grange, set in nearly one hundred acres of land at Farnborough Green, was built in the 1850s by Joseph Timms. Described in the sale particulars as 'a delightfully pretty country house', it was purchased by William Sherwin JP in the mid-1870s. During his ownership a central tower was added over the entrance, which gave it the air of a small stately home. It was later owned by the Holt family during whose time the estate supported a variety of farming activities, including an attempt at strawberry growing in the early 1900s. This was not viable, but a more successful enterprise was Grange Farm Dairies run by the Oakey family. In 1926 the family built a shop in Alexandra Road from where they despatched the daily milk carts across the town.

The Grange itself was used for many years as hostel accommodation for RAE workers but eventually came down to make way for new housing. One part of the Grange Estate still survives in the form of a small lodge on the Farnborough Road, opposite *The Ship*. The

52   Farnborough Grange in the 1950s.

53 Grange Farm Dairies in Alexandra Road.

occupier of the lodge in 1871 was Mr. Edwin McLaurin, who worked as a gardener, winning prizes for his hothouse plants, probably grown in the vast greenhouses attached to the big house. He moved away to become a farm bailiff in Hereford but returned to take over as land steward at Farnborough Hill from his brother Robert Douglas McLaurin who died in 1888.

Chapter Five

Farnborough Hill and the Imperial Connection

The creation of the Farnborough Hill Estate came about during the 1770s when Brigadier Francis Grant acquired the property through a legacy to his wife. The property was then known as Windmill Hill. Brigadier Grant served in America with Lord Howe in 1776, was a Scottish MP for some years and was made a General in 1796. He does not appear to have taken an active interest in local affairs although reference to him can be found in the manorial records in 1775, and in 1780 the marriage of his daughter is recorded in the parish registers. He was, however, a shareholder in the Basingstoke Canal Navigation Company which built the canal in 1778 just to the south of the parish. Perhaps he could see a potential for bringing trade to the area, although in reality the canal had very little effect on the local economy.

In 1806 the property was inherited by his eldest son, James Ludovick Grant, who replaced the old house with a more substantial building.

54 Ordnance Survey map of 1855 showing Windmill Hill.

He also purchased a large amount of land on both sides of the turnpike road which he incorporated into the estate, laying much of it down to the plantation of trees and shrubs. The Grant family was well thought of by the villagers and memorial tablets in the parish church bear witness to this.

The estate was sold in 1819 to Mrs. Mary Foreman, by all accounts a rather eccentric widow who kept her deceased husband's heart in an urn so that it could be buried with her when she died. She obviously liked Farnborough as her will decreed that her remains should be brought back to Farnborough for lying in state at Windmill Hill. On her death, the property was left to her brother, Dr. Chandler, Dean of Chichester, with the exception of the six acres near the station on which she had built a bungalow for her nephew, Edward Greene. This bungalow, known as The Pavilion, she left to Mr. Greene.

Mr. Greene served in the Royal Artillery and was wounded at the Battle of Waterloo in 1815. He retired from the army in 1819 and came to live in Farnborough where he took a great interest in the welfare of the children of both Farnborough and Cove. He purchased some land near the workhouse adjoining the village of Cove, and erected a school called The Oaks. The records commence in 1820 with the formation of a Sunday school, but this quickly converted into a full-time school. Early names on the register are Baigant, Gates, Vollard, Attfield, Bradley, Cranham, Eades and Hall, most of whom can be traced forward for a number of generations. Even as early as 1839, when many early schools were using slates, items in the accounts include cartridge paper, lead for pencils and books for spelling and arithmetic. Two other schools he built were The Beeches, just across Greene's School Lane named in his memory, and Greencroft, further up Victoria Road (and not to be confused with the later Greencroft School in Ship Lane). The Oaks survived until 1967 when it was demolished to make way for a Catholic Parish Centre. There is a small portion of The Beeches still standing as a private house and Greencroft has been replaced with modern flats.

The grounds surrounding Mr. Greene's Pavilion were enlarged when he purchased a further 22 acres from Thomas Longman, the new owner of the Farnborough Hill Estate, in 1860. This was eventually passed on to his own nephew, Mr. Ewen, in 1887. For many years the woodlands were known as Ewen's Woods and were a popular play area for local youngsters. The Pavilion, today known as The

55   The Oaks in the late 1960s.

56 The Pavilion, formerly Mr. Greene's home, in the 1930s when it was named 'The Lodge'.

Lodge and divided into small units, lies in the centre of a modern housing estate called Victoria Court. The surrounding woodland was acquired by the Council in the 1950s for public use as the very popular Queen Elizabeth Park.

Windmill Hill was never occupied by the Dean of Chichester, but the property was let, first to a family called Farquharson about whom little has been recorded, and then to Lady Palmer and her three daughters. Jessie Challacombe recounts, 'The three Misses Palmer were much admired by the village people, especially when they rode about the neighbourhood on horseback. They were considered very grand ladies, and "a bit haughtylike". They were, however, very charitable and it was considered that Lady Palmer only claimed her right when she demanded due deference from the village people.'

When the Dean of Chichester died in 1859, the estate was inherited by his nephew, the Rev. W. Chandler, who immediately sold it to Thomas Longman, the very successful London publisher. The publishing business was doing well and Mr. Longman wanted somewhere out of town but not too far from London for his large family. A sporting man, he knew the area well having hunted there on several occasions. The present Lady Elizabeth Longman owns a painting showing the family enjoying a day's hunting at Farnborough in 1855.

Mr. Longman pulled down the old house and erected a new mansion, designed by Mr. H.E. Kendall, which then became known as Farnborough Hill. A very ornate building of red brick, it is admirably described by Dorothy Mostyn in *The Story of a House*:

> The main block of the building rises from the ground in deep rose brick with stone-mullioned plate-glass windows, as far as the first storey. It then blossoms out into a pattern of teak fleurs-de-lys and arched beams set in pebble-dash, with several beautiful balconies of carved teak supported by stone angels. The square hood moulds around the windows are decorated with delightfully carved corbels representing birds and small animals, such as mice, badgers and monkeys, each in a framework of foliage and fruit or flowers. The pebble-dash is divided from the brick by a frieze of stone-coloured terracotta panels framed in teak, depicting in high relief the various Longman colophons—a ship in full sail, a swan, groups of angels with musical instruments.

It took three years to construct and the family eventually took up occupation in 1863.

Built on the hill, it commanded magnificent views of the surrounding countryside, making it a very popular place for the literary

parties which the Longmans were wont to hold. Writers such as James Froude and Charles Kingsley were frequent visitors, the latter being vicar of Eversley only a few miles away. Mr. Longman created formal gardens near the house, and lovely woodland walks across the turnpike, in what is known today as the Empress Estate.

In the north-west corner of the estate, near Lanes Farm, there were lakes which he stocked with fish. Winters seem to have been a lot colder in those days, when skating parties were held and the nearby boathouse, with its built-in fire-place, provided a warm shelter for the visitors. There are still folk around in the town who remember the ice house, where ice was taken from the frozen lake and stored for use in the summer months. Farnborough Hill Cricket Club was formed in 1861 and the first game was played

57 The Hunt at Farnborough Hill, *c*.1855, showing Thomas Longman and his wife, Mary, with their children who are in the donkey cart. *Reproduced by kind permission of Lady Elizabeth Longman.*

on the cricket field which was situated a short distance from the boathouse. The pattern of summer weather would appear similar to the present day, as heavy rain caused the players to adjourn to the *Tumbledown Dick* to partake of 'a splendid dinner served up by a respected and popular host and hostess of this renowned wayside inn, to which ample justice was done', according to the report in *Sheldrake's Military Gazette*. Some of the early cricketers were Morgan, Fuller, Paul sr, Paul jr, Tugwell, Lloyd sr, Lloyd jr, E. Smith, and Vinson.

The Longman family were extremely benevolent to the villagers. Thomas Longman took an active interest in parish affairs and gave the land for building a village school. The ladies of the family often visited the poor, distributing clothes to the needy and giving parties for the

58 An aerial view of Farnborough Hill in the 1920s. The trees have shielded much of the view today but there is still a magnificent outlook to the east over the old village.

59 The beautiful gardens and ornate features of Farnborough Hill in the early 1900s.

60 Oak Farm in the north west of the parish on the borders of Cove. The original 18th-century farmhouse is just visible behind the Victorian extension at the front. Owned by Mr. A. Hitchcock for many years and then by Mr. Harry Hitchcock, it was originally Lane's Farm but had been re-named Cherrywood when finally sold for demolition.

school children. At Christmas time, the villagers could go up the hill to the 'big house' and receive gifts of food for the festive season. The family was also known to enjoy the plays put on by the local 'mummers' or entertainers.

In 1879 Thomas Longman died and the property was put on the market. It was at this time that the Empress Eugénie, widow of the exiled Napoleon III of France, needed to find a new home. The family had been living in Chislehurst, Kent since they fled France in 1870. The Emperor died in 1873 and in 1879 their son, Prince Louis Napoleon, was tragically killed on active service with the British Army during the Zulu War. His body was returned to England and buried alongside his father in the Catholic Church at Chislehurst.

The Empress wanted to erect a memorial chapel for their tombs and for her own ultimate burial, but was not able to purchase any suitable land. She therefore set about searching for a property elsewhere and eventually decided on Farnborough Hill, where she was also able to acquire some land on a nearby hill for the erection of a chapel.

Although the house had been quite adequate for the needs of the Longman family, Her Imperial Majesty, the Empress Eugénie, considered it to be rather small and she set about enlarging it to suit her needs. By building extensions and making internal alterations she transformed a small country house into an almost palatial mansion with a splendid interior. In March 1884 Queen Victoria made her first visit to Farnborough Hill when she rode over from Windsor with her daughter, Princess Beatrice. The royal party travelled in a landau drawn by four horses and the journey took an hour and a quarter, with a change of horses at Bagshot. After lunching with the Empress, Her Majesty returned to Windsor and noted in her journal that she 'had lunched in a beautiful dining room, at the end of a fine corridor, also entirely built by her & added on'. She also wrote that she had driven into Farnborough Hill past the lodge 'through pretty grounds, up to the house, which looked imposing, with a tower'.

The Empress had a staff of more than twenty-five servants, some of whom had followed the imperial family from France. She treated them well, providing accommodation in houses she built on the estate. While she was at Chislehurst, she was allowed the services of a full-time police officer to guard her and he was paid by the Metropolitan Police Fund. He obviously served her well because, when she moved, she put in a request for the officer, Constable William Tims, to continue his duties at Farnborough. This presented a problem because Constable Tims was an officer in the Metropolitan Police, which covered Chislehurst, and Hampshire was covered by a different police authority. However, as he was on special royal duty, permission was granted and Constable Tims and his family moved to Farnborough and lived in a house on the edge of the estate in Highgate Lane. Ten years later the Metropolitan Police withdrew their funding for the constable, on the grounds of economy. By that time any perceived threats to the Empress' life were probably diminishing, but she continued to employ him privately until he retired.

There were two small lodges attached to the estate, both on the Farnborough Road and both of which are still in use today. The original entrance in Thomas Longman's time, but used today as the exit, was at the northern end and occupied by Xavier Ullman, the Empress' house steward, who had been a batman to the Prince Imperial. The southern lodge, now used as the entrance, was lived in by James Lomas, another

61   The northern lodge at Farnborough Hill in 1916. This was the original entrance to the estate.

62   The southern lodge at Farnborough Hill in the 1930s. Built by the Empress as the new entrance, it stands at the foot of a long and winding drive to the house, bordered on one side by beautiful rhododendrons.

of the Prince's batmen, who acted as lodgekeeper and reputedly wore a 'high top hat and a frock coat which made him look very pompous'.

Once established at Farnborough Hill, the Empress commissioned a French architect, Monsieur Gabriel Hippolyte-Alexandre Destailleur, to build a church and mausoleum. This was commenced in 1883 on the hill directly across the railway from Farnborough Hill and in those days, before the trees grew tall, was easily visible from the Empress' private rooms in the house. Progress was slow and the building was not complete until 1887. Arrangements were then put in hand to transfer the remains of her husband and son to their final resting place.

On 9 January 1888 two coffins containing the remains were lifted from the Church of St Mary's in Chislehurst to a gun carriage and taken in procession to the railway station where a special train was waiting. When the train arrived at Farnborough the coffins were once again placed on gun carriages and drawn by a detachment of the Royal Artillery in procession up to the new church. The cortège was joined by members of the Imperial Household and Major Bigge CB, who represented Queen Victoria. At the chapel, the coffins were transferred into the care of the Abbot Paulin, of the Premonstratensian order of monks who had been installed at the abbey by the Empress to look after the mausoleum. At the end of the service the bodies were laid to rest in the crypt

63 Aerial view of St Michael's Abbey in the 1920s with the entrance drive to Farnborough Hill just visible top right.

64 The arrival of the procession carrying the remains of Napoleon III and the Prince Imperial before their interment at St Michael's Abbey in 1888.

in two large granite sarcophagi, the Emperor being placed on the right and the Prince Imperial to the left of the altar.

In 1895 the Benedictine monks from the French Congregation of Solemnes took over the monastery, and it became an abbey in 1903. The Rt Rev. Dom Ferdnand Cabrol, who had been in charge of the monastery since 1895, became the first abbot. In later years his name was given to one of the roads in the Empress Estate. The Church of St Michael was dedicated in 1908 and the religious community established itself as an integral part of local life. This fact was later to be publicly acknowledged when, in 1934, a coat of arms was granted to the town which incorporated a cross to symbolise a local religious community. The abbey is approached from a driveway leading up from the Farnborough Road. At one time there was a small lodge at the entrance where tickets could be purchased to view the mausoleum. In *Kelly's Trade Directory* of 1889 it advertises that 'The nave is free at times of divine service but a fee of 1s. is charged to view the mausoleum in the afternoon'.

A number of the monks went on active service in the First World War, some receiving military honours. The lay brothers took their

65 The religious ceremony in the crypt, 1888.

66 Coat of Arms granted to the town in 1934 when Farnborough Urban District Council incorporated Cove and parts of Hawley and Minley into its administrative control. The cross at the top represents the religious community of St Michael's. Other features are the Farnborough ferns, the Hampshire rose, the Royal Air Force Wings and the three peaks for the tumuli.

67   Tile Barn House, Prospect Road in the 1960s. Built by the Empress for some of her female staff, it has now been replaced by houses in Tile Barn Close.

part in the efforts to produce food from the land when submarine warfare caused great shortages. By that time the abbey also owned Farnborough Court, built on adjacent land, and this was turned over to the War Department for use as a hospital for wounded Belgian officers. The abbey's connections with the imperial family are still very strong, and occasionally it exhibits its wonderful collection of historic ecclesiastical vestments all beautifully embroidered in rich colours. These include the vestments worn by the monks at the Empress' funeral.

The Empress became a well respected and popular figure who would travel in her carriage to visit the local village, and often went to watch polo matches on the fields opposite the *Queen's Hotel*. A very charitable person, like her predecessor at Farnborough Hill, she also took a great interest in the welfare of the village

children as well as those in nearby Aldershot Camp. She was often seen walking in the grounds of the estate on the western side of the Farnborough Road. Referring to the area as Compiègne, she had redesigned the woodlands and walks to resemble the royal park near Paris. There were swans on the lake, grass tracks, a cycle ride and open spaces where her younger visitors could play games. Apart from the well established trees and rhododendrons, there are few visible signs of this former pleasure ground in the area which now forms the Empress Estate. However, the imperial influence is perpetuated in many of the road names, which reflect her connections with France and the Napoleonic family. Empress Avenue recalls her walk through the woods to Tile Barn, a house she built on Prospect Road for her ladies-in-waiting. Napoleon Avenue and St Michael's Road reflect the family resting place, with Pierrefondes

Avenue representing a favourite place in France. She often used the title Comtesse de Pierrefondes on official documents.

Although the Empress was grateful to have been allowed to live in freedom in this country, she was still drawn to the continent and spent a considerable time cruising around the Medi-terranean. She built a villa on the Riviera and would often travel there in the spring. Distressed by the onset of the First World War, she was anxious to help the French by providing a hospital near her villa but the authorities would not allow it. Instead, she set aside a wing at Farnborough Hill and it was transformed into

68   The Empress with some of the wounded soldiers during the First World War, when part of Farnborough Hill was opened up as a hospital. The patient in the bathchair is F.E. Hill, with Major Mortimer looking on.

69   A snapshot of the monks leading the funeral procession of the Empress as it leaves Farnborough Station for St Michael's Abbey.

a hospital for wounded British officers. The first commandant, in 1914, was Lady Haig, wife of General Sir Douglas Haig, who at the time was living in Combe Farm, near the Clockhouse. Dr. Wilfred Attenborough, a local doctor who lived nearby at The Ridges, acted as medical officer and surgeon. Here the officers were able to convalesce in the peaceful surroundings of the countryside. They were frequently visited by the Empress and were allowed to roam the grounds and even taken out for drives in her motor car.

For her services to the war effort the Empress was decorated by King George V, who sent his two older sons, later to become King Edward VIII and George VI, to invest her with the insignia of a Dame Grand Cross of the British Empire. She had always been held in high regard by the royal family right from the days when she first came across from France

with the Emperor to visit Queen Victoria in the 1850s.

Having been unable to travel to Europe for the duration of the war, at the age of 93 and with failing sight she embarked on a trip to her home in the Mediterranean and then on to Spain. Whilst making preparations to return home, in July 1920, she fell ill and died. Her body was brought back to Farnborough and, in a service attended by the King and Queen, foreign royalty and heads of state from all over Europe, she was interred in the mausoleum alongside her husband and son.

After her death, the Napoleon family did not spend much time in England and only visited Farnborough occasionally for holidays. In 1926 the house at Farnborough Hill was sold to the nuns of Hillside Convent College, who had outgrown their original site at the top of Star Hill on the Farnborough Road. Hillside had been founded in 1889 by the nuns of the Congregation of Christian Education to cater mainly for the daughters of army officers. Their school expanded rapidly and, despite purchasing other houses such as The Sycamores and Wymering Court, the nuns desperately needed more accommodation in order to house both school and boarders under one roof.

The Empress had taken a great interest in the convent over the years and sometimes attended their prize-givings. The children had been allowed to visit Farnborough Hill and enjoyed walking in the woods on the estate. Occasionally, they had been invited to take tea with the Empress. Since her death the house had been well maintained by a small retained staff, so its ninety or so rooms and the magnificent grounds were perfect for immediate occupation by the nuns.

Certain alterations had, of course, to be made to adapt the building for school use; a chapel was built, bathrooms were added, dormitories formed, and much furniture had to be purchased. When the pupils first moved in, conditions were quite spartan but the magnificence and spaciousness of the surroundings were adequate compensation. The contents of the house had been auctioned prior to the sale, but the nuns were able to purchase back some of the lower priced items. Through the years they have been able to acquire other artefacts belonging to the Empress and the influence of the former occupants is still very strong. Pupils have always been encouraged to learn about and develop the history of this very beautiful house, which has a prominent role in the history of Farnborough.

Chapter Six

Village Life

The oldest part of the town lies in an area now known as Farnborough Street. This sometimes causes confusion, as within the village there is a street bearing its name. The nucleus of the old village is centred around the crossroads formed by Highgate Lane, Ship Lane, Farnborough Street and Rectory Road.

It is known that a pottery industry was well established in the vicinity by the 15th century and the earliest maps show dwellings not far from the pottery site at the foot of Farnborough Hill. Part of that site lies under the gardens of properties in a small housing development called Woodstocks. On the

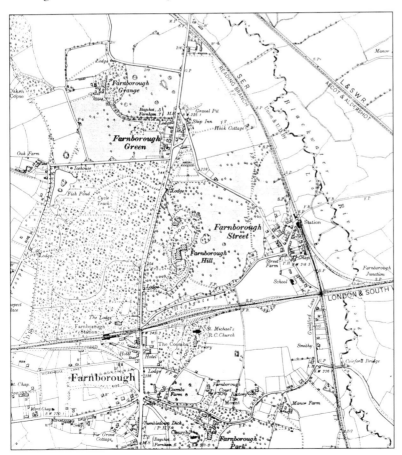

70 Ordnance Survey map of 1898, showing the oldest part of Farnborough.

64

71 Ship Lane Stores in Farnborough Street in the 1950s, formerly the *Rose and Crown*.

right-hand side of Ship Lane, approaching from *The Ship* inn, lies Oriel Cottage, part of which is believed to be an early potter's dwelling. The original timber-framed part on the right of the building is believed to be early 16th-century with later additions in the 19th and 20th centuries. A number of late medieval pottery sherds were found under the floor boards when renovations were being carried out. For many years it was lived in by the Bailiff of Farnborough Hill.

Just a short way along on the right, next door to Empress Cottages, at one time stood an inn called the *Rose and Crown* with a shop adjacent to it. In the 1760s the occupant, John Rowles, was paying a parish rate on the premises. In 1871 it was marked as a public house on the Ordnance Survey map and the census show James Bridger as innkeeper and grocer. Soon afterwards it ceased to be an inn and was run purely as the village shop by the

Bridger family. It was quite a large building with a courtyard and stables at the rear. Many will remember it as Lascelles, which later became Ship Lane Stores, before it was demolished in the 1960s.

Perhaps the best-known building in the centre of the old village is Street Farm. It was probably built in the 17th century, and was considered 'very old' in 1835 when a local potter, William Smith, moved in to it. The story of his life there is well chronicled in *William Smith, Potter and Farmer* by George Bourne, published in 1922. The farmhouse, on the corner of Highgate Lane and Rectory Road, was purchased from the lord of the manor by Thomas Longman in 1860 to become part of the Farnborough Hill Estate. It is now in private hands and divided into four dwellings.

On the adjoining farmland to the west, up Highgate Lane, was a small row of cottages and a potshop belonging to James Callaway.

72   Highgate Lane at the lower corner of Chingford Avenue in the 1930s. The area was once a hop garden leased by William Smith who had his potshop to the left just out of the picture.

This was leased in 1810 by William Smith, who at the age of 19 had learned his trade as a potter in nearby Frimley. He had to work hard to build up his business by selling his wares in London, travelling there regularly to obtain orders. In those early days the goods were transported on the Basingstoke Canal, which seemed a good idea as the condition of the road to London was not good and there were many tolls to pay. However, the canal route proved expensive too, because the goods were first packed carefully onto a cart, taken along the turnpike to the canal at the other end of the parish, then repacked onto the barges only to be unpacked again for their onward journey by cart. William Smith would not entrust the job to anyone else and eventually the task became rather irksome. He reverted to road travel and

was able to recoup some of the costs by hiring the empty carts on the return journey to bring back anything that people wanted to move from London into the country.

The site of the pottery, covered by houses in the 1930s, was almost opposite the footpath which enters the grounds of Farnborough Hill from Highgate Lane. The land next to the pottery, in the area bounded by Chingford Avenue, was once a hopfield and wild hops can still be found growing in the footpath which leads across the railway towards the parish church. There were two other hopfields on the Farnborough Hill Estate, in the area once occupied by the potteries at the northern end of the footpath from Highgate Lane. The adjacent field, which stretched almost up to the big house, was called Windmill Field and, next to that, the land abutting Highgate Lane was known as Potshop Field.

Back in the centre of the village, opposite Street Farm, there is a terrace of three cottages (originally there were four), the left-most one of which housed the first local post office. The fourth cottage in the terrace used to be the Farnborough Dairy owned by Thomas Woods. Next to the dairy was a small building containing one tiny room. This was where Ted Miller had his ladies' and gentlemen's hairdressing business in the 1930s.

Elm Tree House nearby was once overshadowed by a huge pollarded elm tree. This tree was a feature in the lives of the early villagers and tales about it are recounted in Jessie Challacombe's *Jottings from a Farnborough Note Book*. It is even mentioned in the parish records when, in 1797, the accounts include the entry, 'Paid Aaron Brown for repairing the seat round the tree, and painting two gates, £1.0s.9d.' One hundred years later its huge girth was almost hollow, so the local blacksmith, Mr. Bartlett, erected iron railings around it to prevent vagrants sleeping inside. Some residents can still remember the tree being removed by the Council in 1917. Despite being in the middle of a world war, people still found time

73 Ted Miller outside his shop at the junction of Farnborough Street and Rectory Road, *c.*1930.

74 Street Farm and the pollarded elm, *c.*1907.

75   Home Farm in 1968. A small cul-de-sac called Home Farm Close has replaced all the outbuildings and farmyard, but the corner of the old farmhouse, just visible on the left, survives as private housing.

to object, although not on ecological grounds as often happens today, but because it would mean the loss of an historic link with the era when Farnborough lay within Windsor Forest. The only tree comparable in size and antiquity in Farnborough today is a giant chestnut in the gardens of the present Rectory, near the parish church.

The links with Windsor, however, can be found in numerous entries in the parish records which refer to 'Windsor Court rent' being paid until well into the late 1700s. Early maps of Windsor Forest also show the routes of carriage rides accessible from the Castle, namely the Frimley and Lynchford Walks, which converged at the ford across the Black-water River long before North Camp Station was built.

Towards the middle of the 19th century, the lord of the manor took a decreasing role in village affairs and village life centred around the activities at Farnborough Hill. The Home Farm, opposite the old *Rose and Crown*, with its cowsheds, piggery and large stables, belonged to Farnborough Hill and already provided employment for many villagers. The estate had its own fire engine. On one occasion it was sent down to help fight a fire at the *Cambridge Hotel*, when the whole building was destroyed and had to be rebuilt. Another time, whilst fighting a hayrick fire at Home Farm, the pump became clogged with silt from a muddy pond so the villagers had to resort to using buckets of water.

When the army camp was set up in Aldershot, an enterprising brewery, H. & G.

76 Fire pump from Farnborough Hill of the type sometimes called an 'engine'. This one was discovered at Farnborough Hill when some alterations were being carried out and presented to the local Fire Brigade in the 1960s.

77 Sale particulars of *Alma Inn* and other properties in 1860.

Simonds of Reading, realised the potential benefits for their company. Access from Reading was easy via the new Reading, Guildford & Reigate Railway (there being no station yet at North Camp), and by 1856 Mr. Simonds had taken a lease on the *Alma Inn*, on Farnborough Street. Parts of the rear of the inn are considered to be 16th-century, and 17th-century pottery has been found at various times when building work has taken place. It was renamed *The Imperial* when the Empress bought Farnborough Hill.

In 1860 more land became available and Simonds bought the inn and adjoining land and built stables and a large yard. On the opposite side of the road, adjacent to the railway, they built a bottling plant into which the raw materials could be unloaded direct from the trains. From this depot thousands of bottles were despatched by cart to the Camp, which also gave additional employment for the local people. Very quickly, most of the inns and beerhouses in Farnborough came under their name and displayed the company sign of the Hop Leaf. Another bottling depot was later opened in North Camp.

FARNBOROUGH AND YATELY, HANTS,
THE ADJOINING PARISHES OF
FRIMLEY AND ASHE, SURREY.

PARTICULARS
OF THE DESIRABLE

FREEHOLD FARMS & LANDS,
CALLED
"Street Farm," "Lynchford Bridge Farm," and "Lynchford Castle Farm,"

A VALUABLE PUBLIC-HOUSE,
Known as the "Alma Inn,"—Several

DWELLING-HOUSES AND COTTAGES,
With a considerable Extent of

Accommodation, Meadow, and Building Land,
CLOSE TO ALDERSHOT CAMP,

And to the Farnborough and Lynchford Bridge Railway Stations on the London and South Western, and Reading and Reigate Railways,
ALSO, OF

A COPYHOLD ESTATE, CALLED "MITCHET FARM,"
IN THE PARISH OF FRIMLEY, CLOSE TO FARNBOROUGH,
AND

YEALD MOOR, IVELY, AND CLARK'S FARMS, IN YATELY,

For Sale by Auction,
BY

WAINWRIGHTS & HEARD

AT THE "TUMBLE DOWN DICK" INN, FARNBOROUGH STATION,
ON WEDNESDAY, THE 31st DAY OF OCTOBER, 1860,
At Two o'Clock in the Afternoon,

IN THIRTY-ONE LOTS,
Many of which, from their Eligible Situation, afford Advantageous Sites for Building Purposes.

A number of Houses have recently been built in the Neighbourhood, where the Population has greatly increased; and, from the proximity to the Camp, there is a great and growing demand for House Accommodation and for Business Premises.

The Property may be viewed on application to the Tenants, or MR. CARTER, at the "Tumble Down Dick" Inn, (who will send a person to shew it.) Particulars of the Lots may be obtained at the Place of Sale, of MR. AMOS YATES, of North Camp, of MESSRS. ATTWOOD & RIGDEN, Surveyors, Salisbury, of WAINWRIGHTS & HEARD, Surveyors, Shepton Mallet, Somerset, or of

MESSRS. NEWMAN, LYON AND NEWMAN,
Solicitors, 7, King's Bench Walk, Temple, London, and Yeovil, Somerset.

PRINTED AT THE STEAM PRESS OFFICE, YEOVIL.

78 H. & G Simonds' yard at
Farnborough North Station in
1909. Mr. William Beck is the
second drayman from the right.
The gas holder for the estate is
tucked behind the stables and
the old laundry chimney can be
seen on the left, behind the
Home Farm buildings.

79   Fred Ede, on the left, with assistant Bob Allum in the 1930s.

80   Yew Tree Cottage, Farnborough Street, early 1900s.

More village shops sprang up along The Street. Next to *The Imperial* was Mr. Ede, the 'snob', the old name for a boot and shoe repairer. He had a tiny shop with steps up to it and a room out the back. This has now been incorporated into the adjacent house called Cobblers Cottage and Yew Tree Cottage is next door to that. Opposite was a terrace of four old cottages where some of the Simonds' workers used to live but these were demolished many years ago. Opposite *The Imperial* was a bakery owned at one time by Mr. Gates where, according to Jessie Challacombe, 'all the baking was done on a Sunday in the early days for it was the custom to send the Sunday joint and potatoes to be cooked at the bakehouse, whilst the family went to church. Dinner was then ready when the service was over.' A Methodist church was built on the site in 1952. That building has now been converted into a veterinary centre.

Alongside the old church is a pathway leading to Chapel Street, at the far end of which is the early Primitive Methodist Chapel built in 1866. Constructed at a cost of £53 10s. 10d., on a plot of land bought for £10, its leading light was Mr. M. Ray who worked for the London & South Western Railway. He lived in the house attached to the chapel. The records show that the chapel was opened on 8 July 1866 amidst great rejoicing; a marquee was hired for the occasion and a sizeable collection for those days of £7 13s. 0d. was recorded. When the new church was built, the former chapel became a church hall until it was sold to a local builder. Next to the chapel was a large field which belonged to Mr. Compton, who owned the *Prince of Wales* public house in Rectory Road. Many fairs and fêtes were held in this field and the entertainment was sometimes provided by Billy Matthews, a local fairground operator who lived in North Camp.

Early education in the village was courtesy of a Mrs. Cook, who had once been a ladies' maid at the Manor House. Known as Dame Cook, she taught the children in a schoolroom attached to her cottage. Today, halfway along

81 A painting of the Primitive Methodist Chapel and House in Chapel Street by local artist David Pritchard, compiled with the aid of photographs and personal memories of a family who lived in the Chapel House for many years.

82 The Old School House is seen left of centre behind the goal in this photograph of the North Farnborough Football Club in 1952. The bungalows had yet to be built on this part of the Rectory Road Recreation Ground.

83   The children of Class V at Farnborough National School, Rectory Road in 1912.

Rectory Road, between the railway bridge and Coleford Bridge Road, there is a white painted house with a large garage attached to the right-hand side. That garage is the old schoolroom. The room was divided by a wooden bench and the story is told in *A Farmer's Life* by George Sturt of how the older boys would stand on the bench to look out of the window and watch the cattle drinking at the nearby pond, half-way between the school and the railway bridge. It is difficult to imagine the road before the embankment was constructed, but school records show that flooding was often the reason children were absent in winter. Jessie Challacombe also recounts that, when the first

trains went by, the schoolchildren were taken along to watch the spectacle.

Dame Cook retired in 1864 so the church rented the schoolroom and employed a school-master to continue teaching there. Soon the premises became far too small and, through the generosity of Thomas Longman of Farnborough Hill, who provided the land, a new National School was built in the village. The old school building was bought by Mr. Bartlett, who ran his blacksmith's business from there until 1900 when he moved to premises nearer the railway bridge.

The National School was opened in 1868 and Mr. Longman's daughters often used to visit the school to listen to the children reading. The rector was another regular visitor and took an active part in the school management. When the Empress Eugénie became the new owner of Farnborough Hill, she too used to visit the children and sometimes took tea with them. She also allowed them to go walking in the grounds of Farnborough Hill. In 1905 the infants were transferred to the North Farnborough County Infant School in a new building next door. The National School became St Peter's Junior School in 1939 and moved into its present home at Farnborough Place in 1962.

Next to the playground of the infants school there is a white house which has recently been converted from a shop. This became the post office and village shop some time around the beginning of the 20th century and remained as such for nearly eighty years, before the post office moved again to another site in Highgate Lane. Adjacent to the house is a row of 1930s houses which replaced the very pretty Laburnum Cottages, so named after a beautiful old laburnum tree in the front garden.

The villagers had quite a long walk to the parish church, particularly those who lived in the cottages near Hook Farm on the Blackwater River, now part of Farnborough Gate retail site. The farm took its name from the bend or hook in the river which is shown on very early maps. An ancient path led across the fields, through what is now Farnborough Hill, across Highgate Lane, and through the

84   Decorations for the coronation of King George V outside the post office in Rectory Road, next door to Laburnum Cottages.

85   The Chapel and Hearse House in Victoria Road Cemetery, erected in 1859.

86   Memorial to Queen Victoria in Victoria Road Cemetery, as it was in 1960.

glebelands to the church. The railway had made a deep cutting through the glebelands, so it is easy to see why the parish elders insisted on the provision of a footbridge before allowing the railway across the land.

By 1859 the villagers had even further to walk to the new cemetery which was opened on the road to Cove. The tiny parish church-yard was full due to the large number of military burials which took place after the Crimean War. Many of the soldiers returning to their base in North Camp died of their wounds and had to be buried in Farnborough as the Camp was within the parish boundary.

The local Burial Board, consisting of prominent local inhabitants, found a suitable plot but had to negotiate for its purchase. The land was owned by Mr. Morant and rented to Mary Hall, who had to be paid compensation to move out. The Board borrowed £700 from the government, repayable over thirty years,

and plans were drawn up for the construction. Contracts were awarded for various aspects of the project, including the planting of the holly hedge and seeding of the grounds. A small chapel was erected by local builder, David Smith of Frimley, and the fencing was done by Reuben Yates, one of the first traders in North Camp. Mr. Bridger of Farnborough Street provided much of the building material. The chapel itself cost £283 to build, the remainder of the money being spent on landscaping, fencing, fees and the purchase costs.

By 1898 the new cemetery faced a new overcrowding problem because of the huge expansion in the town's population, so additional land on the Union Street side was acquired. The original northern boundary fence of holly remains as a line of now mature trees dividing the two sections. In the centre of the cemetery lies a memorial to Queen Victoria, who died on 22 January 1901 after reigning for 64 years.

She had been a frequent visitor to the town, both as sovereign to review her troops, and as friend to the exiled Empress Eugénie.

Victoria Road, once a track leading from the village of Cove and also known as New Road, gradually developed into a shopping area serving the northern part of the town. Almost opposite the cemetery is the *Alexandra* public house. Originally a cottage with a butchery attached, referred to in the 1871 census as the Victoria Beerhouse, it was eventually taken over by Simonds Brewery. One of the earliest businesses was Spooner's forge, almost opposite the end of Elm Grove Road, now just a memory. Adrian Job Spooner had been apprenticed to Mr. Bartlett of Farnborough Street but he took over the farrier's business of

Mr. Instone, who wanted to concentrate on his wheelwright's shop in Cove. The Spooners remained in business until the late 1960s, by which time the demand for shoeing horses in the area had greatly diminished.

The row of shops opposite Spooner's, known as The Broadway, was where Williamson's, a very popular grocery, started up in the early 1900s. They specialised in cheeses, bacon and tea, and, like many of the other traders, delivered daily to local customers. The greengrocer's next door was Hedger's, and Webb the butcher was beyond, with a small slaughterhouse at the rear of the premises.

Just around the corner, on the Farnborough Road, was another row of shops near the *Tumbledown Dick*. Here, in Park Terrace,

87 Inside Williamson's shop in Victoria Road, *c.*1930s.

was another butcher, Mr. J. Swain, who had a double-fronted shop. He also had a slaughterhouse for killing and curing his own animals, which were then hung up both inside and outside to attract customers. The shop had wide open windows, exposing the meat to all the dust from the road. There was no pavement then and the road was little more than sand and gravel. In dry weather the Council sent round the water cart to spray the roads to keep down the dust, but the system was neither frequent nor effective. It was not uncommon, then, for butchers and dairymen to appear before the local magistrates for selling contaminated food. Alongside Mr. Swain was the post office, a haberdasher and a fishmonger. Park Terrace was demolished in the 1970s to make way for the Kingsmead multi-storey car park.

There has been an inn on the site of the *Tumbledown Dick* for many centuries. Documentary evidence as to its exact age is inconclusive but maps of the 16th and 17th centuries clearly show an inn. It is noted in the 1825 sale documents of Farnborough Park, on land owned by the lord of the manor, as having been built around 1817, when William Pryor took on a lease for 12 years. Folklore attributes the name to the downfall of either Richard III, Richard Cromwell or even Dick Turpin, who is reputed to have slept there. Another plausible, if fanciful, legend appears in *Traditions about Aldershot* by Charles Stanley Herve, published in 1865. It recounts that a local lad named Dick Thrupples, who had been crippled by an accident in childhood, used to drink with two friends at an inn called the *Duke of Cumberland*. He was often teased and

88   Swain's butcher's shop at Nos. 4 and 5 Park Terrace, Farnborough Road, *c*.1910.

Tumble Down Dick Hotel,

FARNBOROUGH, Hants.

Proprietor : G. W. STEELE.

89 An advertisement for the *Tumbledown Dick*, 1911.

one day someone weakened the leg of his chair causing him to fall and slide under the table. The landlord was so amused he commissioned a painting to record the event. In due course, Dick Thrupples is supposed to have bought the inn and changed its name to the *Tumbledown Dick*. The author of the tale warns that he had occasionally changed names to protect individuals, but in one of George Sturt's local biographies, *A Farmer's Life*, his uncle vaguely recalled a sign which depicted a man with a pipe and glass falling under a table. Whatever the origin of the name, the *Tumbledown Dick* has managed to survive, although it is gradually being dwarfed by surrounding developments.

Chapter Seven

North Camp

In 1853 the government, encouraged by Queen Victoria and Prince Consort Albert, took the decision to build a permanent camp at Aldershot for the training of the army. In 1854 the land was purchased and plans were drawn up to erect wooden barracks on the east side of the turnpike road, now the Farnborough Road. The area between the Basingstoke Canal and Aldershot was known as South Camp, with North Camp being on the northern side of the Basingstoke Canal up as far as Lynchford Road. Most of North Camp, therefore, lay on wasteland within the parish of Farnborough. A proportion of this wasteland had been allocated under the Enclosure Acts to the poor, who were allowed to cut a small amount of turf each year for fuel. The £2,000 paid by the government for the land was invested in stocks, with some of the income being allocated for the provision of coal for the poor.

By May 1854 a number of wooden huts had been erected in North Camp ready to receive the first soldiers, who came from the 94th Regiment based in Windsor. The urgency of preparing the camp for the influx of military personnel necessitated employing many civilians to undertake the construction work. Labourers walked many miles each day to obtain this lucrative work, and enterprising shopkeepers set up businesses on Lynchford Road to help them spend their money.

The first merchants traded out of hastily erected wooden huts, but as fire was a perpetual hazard more permanent structures quickly followed. One fire reported in *Sheldrake's Military Gazette* in 1863 broke out on North Camp Green, at the blacksmith's forge occupied by Mr. Instone. This was behind the shops where Peabody Road car park is today. The fire spread quickly through the wooden buildings but major destruction was prevented when the Military Fire Brigade arrived from the Camp, bringing two engines and a number of fire screens. The engines were hand-operated pumps on horse-drawn carts. The screens blocked the flames to prevent them spreading, and with the aid of water pumped from a nearby muddy horsepond the fire was put out. Although Mr. Badger, the mineral water manufacturer, lost his stables, the horses were rescued. However, Mr. Amos Yates, the forage contractor, lost his entire stock of wood and railway sleepers which had been stored outside his premises, near what is now the *Elephant and Castle*.

Amos Yates had been one of the first traders to move in to North Camp. He purchased a large piece of land fronting Lynchford Road and built his house where the old Kingdom Hall of Jehovah's Witnesses now stands. Many people will remember it as Silver's fish shop. During a shopping festival in the 1930s, one elderly resident recounted to the *Aldershot News* that it used to be a 'pretty cottage with a lawn in front and covered in wisteria'. Immediately adjacent is a narrow lane now leading to the car park which used to be called Yates' Alley, leading to Yates' Yard.

Other articles printed in the *Aldershot News* during the 1930s, recalling memories of the previous fifty years, give more interesting

90   Soldiers marching along Lynchford Road before turning down the Queen's Avenue in 1907. They have just passed the *Elephant and Castle* and are heading towards the *North Camp Hotel*.

information about the early traders. One such reads:

> The first building activities were connected with the military and took the form of a series of stables built to the north of Lynchford Road. To the west, where is now Morris Road, was a gravel pit from which was dug much of the gravel used for road making in the camp. When the gravel was exhausted, the site was used as a piggery, and the residents in those days found it great fun to assist the owner of 200 porkers when the latter showed a disinclination to pass through the entrance gates, which were close to the premises occupied now by Mr. H.J.E. Brake, whose father was one of the pioneers of Farnborough. Sixty years ago it was almost possible to count on two hands the number of buildings in Lynchford Road. From a wooden bungalow known as Stent Cottage, midway between Alexandra Road and Camp Road, it was a short stroll to the next building, the *Barley Mow* public house, which now has another title. Behind this was eventually erected Farnborough's own theatre or music hall as it was termed in those days. Beyond the *Barley Mow* was a grocers, then a bungalow and a mineral water factory where the machinery was operated, even in those early days, by horse power, but in this case a blind horse which spent its days tramping a circle until its daily work was done. Mr. Badger was the proprietor of the factory. Beyond the factory were two cottages and then the *Blacksmith's Arms*, a residence in which Mr. Clem Yates, to whom we are indebted for much of the information in this article, was born—by coincidence only a few yards from his present premises.

From the foregoing it would seem likely that the *Barley Mow* was on the site of the present *North Camp Hotel*, and the *Blacksmith's Arms* could well have been the forerunner of the *Elephant and Castle* public house. What is also interesting is that many of those early recollections can be borne out by looking at census returns, parish records and trade directories of the day. The parish rate books first record the shops in North Camp in 1856.

It is difficult to imagine the sheer numbers of soldiers in the vicinity in those early days, but a report in the *Illustrated London News* of 1858, describing the visit of Queen Victoria, is a good guide:

> The long deferred visit of the Queen to the military camp at Aldershott took place on Tuesday week. The troops were paraded at nine o'clock in their active service full marching order, and before ten o'clock the whole force was marching towards Frimley in four brigades, each formed into continuous columns. The whole division consisted of eleven regiments of infantry, two regiments of cavalry, twenty four guns, a detachment of engineers, and a battalion of the Military Train, in all about 12,000 or 13,000 men—a very respectable force to move with facility even for a few miles along a turnpike road. The column took the direct route along the Winchester Road, passing through the camp across the railway bridge at the Farnborough station of the South Western line through Farnborough and Frimley to Frimley Green, upon the advance guard reaching which place, the whole column, which extended for several miles along the road, halted to await the arrival of the Royal party ...
>
> ... the column of troops was again set in motion and marched past the Queen's carriage without carrying arms or dipping the colours; in fact, in exactly the same order as if on a long march. The appearance of the troops in heavy marching order, incumbered by all the useful but inelegant accessories of active service, if not so gay as when on parade, is infinitely more martial, and impresses the spectator with the idea that he is witnessing a really effective military force and not a mere holiday procession. The discipline of the troops seemed admirable; regiment after regiment, as they rounded the inclosure and defiled past the Staff, stepping as one man, showed the strict training they had been under, and the advantages of teaching the troops to act together, not in regiment but in large brigades and divisions. After passing through Frimley the column struck into a cross road and after making a circuit of a couple of miles again formed on the main road to the camp, a little beyond the Farnborough station. After the passing of the rear guard the Royal party drove rapidly in the direction of the camp, again meeting the head of the column as it merged upon the Aldershott Road. The cortège took up their station on the edge of Cove common where it remained until the troops had filed past a second time, which second inspection did not terminate until about half past two o'clock.

The large influx of soldiers requiring food and entertainment opened the door to the establishment of more beerhouses, provision merchants, saddlers, tailors and ironmongers. At one time there were seven boot and shoe makers in Lynchford Road alone as well as the businesses springing up in Camp, Peabody and Queen's Roads nearby. A popular beerhouse with the soldiers was the *Fir Tree* at North Camp Station. This was opened in 1862, when the landlord, Mr. L. Monoghan, placed an advertisement in the local press announcing that he had obtained a wines and spirit licence and could sell a wide variety of beers. Reputed to have been used as a ticket office for the horse-drawn trams, it remained a public house until the 1990s when falling business caused it to be closed and it was sold for commercial use.

In a camp made up of tents and wooden huts, there was nowhere for visiting dignitaries or senior army officers to stay. In about 1855 the *Queen's Hotel* was erected at the junction of Lynchford Road and Farnborough Road. Believed to have been built by a Mr. Hemmings, it was a large wooden building with verandas, containing many rooms, and enjoying excellent views over the Camp and across the Common.

The land was originally purchased by William Knell, an early developer in Farnborough, who leased the adjacent tap and stables to a Mr. Taunton in 1860. In 1861 the fledgeling Farnborough and Aldershot Freehold and Ground Rent Society became involved, although Mr. Knell was still paying a parish rate on the property in 1867. In 1885 a company called The Queen's Hotel and Sanatorium Ltd. was formed to purchase the hotel together with 'the taps, stables, rink and other pleasure grounds'. Before they could make the purchase they had to apply to the Home Office for permission to include the word 'Queen's' in their title as it inferred a royal connection. Their application stated that the hotel had traded under that name for many years, had been patronised by the royal family as well as a great many officers, and the business would suffer greatly if the name were altered. Their request was granted. The taps were the beer drinking areas open to the general public, and the rink was a roller skating rink on the land immediately to the north of the site between Farnborough Road and Southampton Street.

In the early days, the *Queen's Hotel* was in a prime position to view the Aldershot Camp Races which took place on the Queen's Parade. The first meeting was held in 1860 and was such a success that the following year the traders

of Farnborough presented the organisers with The Farnborough Cup, valued at 100 guineas, for one of the races. People came in their carriages from great distances causing quite a traffic jam near the hotel. Stands were erected for the spectators, entertainers performed and there were sideshows and stalls, all creating a colourful event which by all accounts could rival Epsom Races. In later years polo was another popular sport, and participants stayed at the hotel. The Command Polo Club was occasionally favoured with visits from the Prince of Wales, who was able to play in matches in the comparative privacy of the garrison fields.

The hotel was rebuilt in the 1880s and again in 1903 following a disastrous fire. The Edwardian building we see today, once known across the world by every officer who had served in the British Army, has rather lost its identity in the ever-changing world of business hotel chains. Nevertheless, whatever corporate name it is given, it will always remain 'The Queen's' in the hearts of Farnborough people.

Another early trader in Lynchford Road was Mr. Arthur Turner, who started his business as a general dealer and furniture maker in 1872. This soon expanded, as indicated by his entry in the 1889 edition of *Kelly's Directory* which

F. RICHTER, Manager.

Telephone: No. 4 North Camp.
Telegrams: "Queen's," South Farnborough.

91 The *Queen's Hotel, c.*1910.

R.A.C.   A.A.   C.V.M.

QUEEN'S HOTEL, FARNBOROUGH

TELEPHONE : FARNBOROUGH 1000

THE QUEEN'S HOTEL, Farnborough is recognised as the premier hotel of the great Army and Air Force centre of Aldershot and Farnborough, and the Hotel has a particularly pleasant situation among the avenues between the two centres. It is nearest for both, and close to the Officers' Club and the grounds for polo, tennis and other sports.

The Hotel is the nearest one for the Tattoo ground, and the golf course on Farnborough Common is opposite the Hotel. Several other famous links such as Sunningdale, Bramshill, Woking, and Camberley being within a short distance.

Within easy access are such places as Ascot, Windsor, Henley and the beautiful country round Guildford and Hindhead.

The Queen's Hotel has been recently renovated and re-decorated and has a full range of public rooms and bedrooms, and its own gardens and tennis courts.

92 Tariff for the *Queen's Hotel* just before the Second World War.

93 Arthur Turner, one of the early traders in North Camp.

TARIFF

Bed, Breakfast and Bath per night per person   .   from **8/6**
En Pension   .   .   .   .   . from **3½** Gns. per week.
Table d'hote Luncheon **3/-**
Afternoon Tea **1/6**
Dinner **4/6**
also à la carte---English Grill.

The terms do not apply to the period of the Aldershot Tattoo.

Hot and Cold Running Water in all Bedrooms.
Central Heating. — Gas Fires in Bedrooms. — Free Car Park.
Private Lock-ups. — Spacious Ballroom. — Banquetting Rooms.

En Pension Terms must be claimed at time of Booking or full
Tariff Rates will be charged.

Proprietors : H. & G. SIMONDS, LTD., The Brewery, READING.

Vulcan Press.   The R.A.P. Co. Ltd.. London, E.C.4.

reads, 'Turner, Arthur, timber merchant, builder, undertaker, monumental mason, iron-monger, wholesale oil & colour merchant, cabinet maker, furniture dealer, china, glass & earthenware dealer and general stores, Lynchford Road, North Camp'. His premises were on the corner of Peabody Road where the family business remained for nearly a century.

Many of the traders who set up in Aldershot to serve the South Camp started to branch out into North Camp. Thomas White opened up a department store on the corner of Camp Road selling everything from camp cooking equipment to cots and prams, clothes and furniture. The wooden structure was three storeys high, with a huge sign standing above the roof. This advertising strategy was used by some of the traders so that their business could be seen from right across the Camp.

All the shops and businesses were erected on the north side of Lynchford Road, facing the camp. The only buildings on the south side

were for military use. Many of the locals likened this situation to that of seaside resorts, where the shops face the sea; they would refer to the shopping area as 'along the front'. Gradually more houses and businesses appeared in the adjoining Alexandra, Camp, Queen's and Peabody Roads. White's trade increased so much that by 1897 they had to construct a much larger shop on their site, providing a department store which served the town well into the middle of the 20th century. Over the years it, too, suffered disastrous fires, resulting in the present rather bland building that is now occupied on the ground floor by a motorcycle clothing retailer.

As the number of buildings in the civilian part of North Camp grew the fire risk increased. Gradually a form of voluntary fire fighting evolved, but it was not until the early 1890s that there was a structured volunteer fire brigade. By 1898 they had acquired their first fire engine, a horse-drawn vehicle with a large steam-driven

94 An illustration which appeared in the *Aldershot News* in 1897 showing White's new premises on the corner of Camp Road.

95 The Popular Restaurant, Camp Road in 1930 offered 'popular prices' such as sausage and chips for 10d. and a packet of 10 cigarettes for 4d. Miss Barton, whose father owned the restaurant, is on the left.

pump attached to a tank of water. There was no proper fire station such as the army had in Queen's Avenue, but the volunteers were able to use an old wooden shed in Camp Road for housing the engine. By 1905 the wooden shed was falling into disrepair and the engine was deteriorating, so the Council agreed to build a fire station adjacent to the new Town Hall.

Although still a volunteer service, the men took their job very seriously. They trained rigorously to become more proficient and entered competitions with other local brigades, often winning prestigious cups. The Council, ever mindful of having to justify its expenditure, ordered regular exercises to monitor the brigade's progress. These tests established the time taken for the men to arrive from their place of work and how quickly they could hitch up the horse, fire the boiler to get up steam, and arrive at the fire with hoses ready for action. Eight to nine minutes was a fair average when attending fires in North Camp.

96 Aerial view of North Camp in the early 1920s clearly showing the concentration of civilian buildings on the north of Lynchford Road, with the barrack squares and military quarters to the south.

97 Farnborough Fire Brigade's first engine, *c.*1905.

98 Fire-damaged house in Alexandra Road, *c*.1909. Local builders Metherell & Harvey erected scaffolding to enable them to repair the severely damaged roof. All the members of the Volunteer Fire Brigade took the opportunity to pose for one of their own men, Mr. D. Lawrence, to take this photograph.

Expanding businesses brought banking services to the area. The London and County Bank built an impressive branch on the corner of Alexandra and Lynchford Roads in 1898. Prior to that, the bank manager in Aldershot had to travel by horse and trap to visit his customers in North Camp. London and County has now evolved into NatWest but still retains its prominence in today's vastly scaled down shopping area. Lloyds Bank, formerly Capital and Counties, was just around the corner in Lynchford Road, where their large premises contained two shops in the front of the building, the bank entrance being on the corner of

Church Path. Over the years the shops disappeared as, with their own expanding business, the bank required the whole of the building. Despite the commercial and military decline of that part of the town, it too has survived and is a reminder of a prosperous period of the town's development. In the ensuing years two other banks, National Provincial and Midland, opened in Alexandra Road but both have now closed, as has the Trustee Savings Bank in Camp Road.

Immediately behind Lloyds Bank there was, until a few years ago, the Wesleyan School. It opened in 1877 and was attended by both military and civilian children. Enlarged in 1884 and 1886, it had an average attendance nearing 350 when overcrowding necessitated the building of the Queen's Road Council School in 1912. Built on the edge of an old gravel pit, the new school provided more spacious accommodation, including a large assembly hall where many dramatic productions were staged by the pupils. Their headmaster, Mr. Miller, was a keen musician who also encouraged sporting activities and the school won many prizes in local competitions. In the 1930s there was an annual carnival in the town, and the school usually won a prize for its entry.

As the population in North Camp and South Farnborough rapidly increased, so came a proliferation of privately run schools. Farn-

99 Capital and Counties Bank buildings in Lynchford Road in 1911, when John Farmer Shoe Company and Eastman & Son Cleaners shared the frontage. The entrance to the Wesleyan Hall was in the centre, where the main entrance to Lloyds Bank is today.

100 Queen's Road School Class 4B's entry for the Farnborough Carnival in the mid-1930s.

101   South Farnborough High School in Reading Road, early 1920s.

102   The tower that was never built at St Mark's Church, from an architect's sketch which appeared in the parish magazine in 1896.

borough School, Hillside Convent, Pinewood, Belgrave and Crossways occupied large buildings around the northern end of Alexandra Road. To begin with these schools generally catered for the children of officers destined for public schools, but one small private school for local children was South Farnborough High School. It started life in a private house in Lynchford Road run by two sisters, the Misses Hall. They subsequently purchased a house called Hazeldene, in Reading Road, and transferred their school to the new premises. The house has now been extended and is used as a nursery school.

A few yards away, opposite the old Town Hall, is the church of St Mark. Once South Farnborough began to develop, the number of parishioners grew at such an alarming rate that the facilities of the parish church were rather over-stretched. It was felt that the spiritual needs of this end of the town would be better served by a chapel of ease with a curate in charge. Thus, in 1878, at a meeting held in The Sycamores, the home of Sir Thomas McMahon, the decision was taken to build St Mark's Church. The intention was to build the church, a house for the curate and a school, but the school was eventually built in Queen's Road. In July 1880 the foundation stone of the church was laid by the Duchess of Connaught. The original design had allowed for a tower but this was never built, although the base section was constructed in 1889. A glance into the cupboard inside the entrance lobby reveals the foot of a stone staircase going nowhere!

In 1878 the Aldershot Orphanage was opened in Alexandra Road under the charge of Mr. and Mrs. Pashly. It was a large, red-brick building capable of housing about a hundred children. From the 1881 census it is easy to establish that the children were mainly from army families. In 1898 the orphanage was extended and a large number of boys were transferred from the Children's Home in Gravesend, Kent. Schooling was provided and the headmaster tried to create a family atmosphere in the residential accommodation, although conditions were not always very satisfactory. Eventually it became a branch of the National Children's Home and Orphanage, but with only voluntary funds to support them the buildings fell into disrepair and the Home closed in 1953. The Council then took over the premises for use as additional administrative offices. When the new Council Offices were built in 1981 the main part of the building was

103 St Mark's Church in the 1920s, when much of Alexandra Road was still covered in trees.

104   Children's Home and Orphanage in Alexandra Road in the early years of the 20th century.

demolished to make way for a development called Wetherby Gardens. The remaining buildings are either offices or private apartments.

There was another orphanage nearby in Queen's Road. Once again, the occupants were army children and it was known as the Soldiers' Boys Home. The building, on the corner of Queen's Road and Sherborne Road, had originally been a tin factory where pots and pans were manufactured. The 1881 census shows it in the occupation of Mr. Thomas Ward, along with his family, a few tinplate workers and a large number of young boys. Mrs. Ward is shown as the matron and there

are more tinplate workers in nearby cottages. By the end of the 1890s, the demand for tin-ware had declined and Mr. Ward had moved to Lynchford Road, but forty boys were still in residence when the building was sold to the Salesian Fathers in 1901.

By 1903 the church of Mary Help of Christians was built adjoining the home to serve the Salesian Community and the local Catholic population. Salesian Sisters arrived to care for the domestic arrangements and gradually a school emerged which eventually became an independent grammar school. The Sisters went on to teach in the parish primary school of St Patrick's which started in Peabody Road and eventually moved to Whitefriars in Avenue Road. As the Salesian School celebrates its centenary, the old tin factory has been demolished and a new church has been erected in its place.

The college playing fields in Park Road were acquired in 1911. In earlier years this was the training ground for some of Farnborough's first star footballers. In 1898 Farnborough won the Aldershot and District Combination League with a team which included Archie Turner, who went on to play for Southampton and England. At the end of his football career he returned to the family business started by his grandfather Arthur Turner. Many members of the team came from the families of local traders, including 'Tintoe' Jones, a well-known builder so named because his football skills were attributed to his 'tin' toes, and Frank Harmsworth from the boatyard at Ash.

Law and order among the soldiers was enforced by the military police stationed in the Camp. Civilian policing was more difficult as the constables were stationed in police houses around the town. In 1898 a police station was built next door to the London and County Bank, on Lynchford Road, and the police families moved to the new adjacent quarters. The modern station had cells for miscreants and was also equipped with one of the first telephones in Farnborough; it had the number of North Camp No. 6.

In 1895 the National Telephone Co. Ltd. installed a public telephone call office in the premises of the Aldershot Dairy Supply Association in Lynchford Road. The number was 501 because, although this was the first telephone in Farnborough, the North Camp exchange lines came within the Reading area of the telephone company and the prefix '5'

105   The Salesian School on the corner of Sherborne Road in 1911. The part of the building on the Queen's Road frontage was a former tin factory and then an orphanage.

106 South Farnborough Football Club, winners of the Aldershot and District Combination Shield in 1899, on the grounds in Park Road where they used to do their training. From left to right on the back row: R. Paice, J.H. Paice, Hon. Sec., G.V. Thomas, W. Searle, A. Turner, International, and H. Davis, Trainer. On the middle row: P. Robinson, H.E. Robinson, F.C. Paice. On the front row: C. Yorker, A. Roberts, F. Harmsworth, H. Turner and T. Jones.

107 The Police Station and its quarters, Lynchford Road, as they were in 1971.

FARNBOROUGH.

8	BROWN, T.		Butcher and Poulterer	Lynchford road.
10	DARRACOTT, Thos.		Confectioner	Lynchford road.
12	DREW, J.		Printer and Stationer	Lynchford road.
21	FOSTER & Wells		Solicitors	Alexandra road.
6	HAMPSHIRE County Constabulary			Police station.
24	JOHNSON, J. F. & Co.	Architects, Estate Agents		Lynchford road.
3	JUNIOR Army and Navy Stores	General Traders		Queen's road.
22	MAY, Jas.		Printer	Lynchford road.
1	NATIONAL Telephone Co., Ld.			1, Morris road.
19	OVER, R. & P.	Drapers, House Furnishers		Cove road.
5	PATERSON, C. E.		Physician	Stirling lodge, Alexandra road.
17	PERRYMAN, C. W.			Bifrons.
50	POST Office (for Postal facilities **ONLY**)			
4	QUEEN'S Hotel			
16	RAMILLIES Barracks (Royal Dublin Fusiliers)			
7	RATCLIFFE, Jesse		Butcher, Game Dealer	Lynchford road.
18	RATCLIFFE, Jesse		Butcher and Dairyman	Farnborough road.
20	SIMONDS, H. & G., Ld.		Brewers	Queen's road.
23	SMITH, Wm.		Builder and Contractor	
14	SPROT, Major A.			The Firs.
11	WALLIS, E.		Grocer	Lynchford road.
9	WHITE, Thomas & Co.			Lynchford road.

108 Extract from telephone directory of 1897.

109 Branson's tobacconist's, Camp Road in the early 1930s, soon after it was built. Although no longer in the ownership of the original family, it is one of the few shops in North Camp to have retained its original identity.

was the exchange code. In 1897 the telephone company took a lease on No. 1 Morris Road and installed another public phone in the front room of what was then probably a small shop. This became the telephone exchange, where the telephone operator would connect the calls with the fast-expanding countrywide telephone system. The number was transferred to No. 1 Morris Road and the original call office was transferred to the offices of James May, the printer in Lynchford Road. The houses in Morris Road have since been renumbered, but in those days No. 1 was the first house in the small terrace on the Lynchford Road side of Andorra Terrace. In 1899 the exchange came under the management of the Guildford Area and the numbers lost their 5 prefix. Morris Road remained the local exchange until 1928, when a new telephone exchange with some 600 lines was opened on the Farnborough

Road, at the junction with Reading Road. During the early 1920s all the numbers took on the name of either North or South Farnborough but by the end of the decade they had became Farnborough numbers. This caused one local councillor to wonder whether the exchange should have the word 'Hants' added, to distinguish it from towns of the same name in Kent, Warwickshire and Berkshire, but by that time the Hampshire town had grown to such an extent it was considered important enough not to need any added identification.

North Camp was for many years the commercial centre of the town but it began to lose its importance with the decline in the military population during the 1960s. This coincided with the building of a new town centre shopping complex on the Queensmead/ Kingsmead site at the northern end of the town.

Chapter Eight

From Kites to Concorde

Farnborough today is world renowned for its Air Show and its connection with the development of aviation. This chapter in its history began when the Army Balloon Factory moved from Aldershot to Farnborough in 1905. Part of the old building from the Royal Engineers' balloon site in Aldershot was re-erected on the common on the western side of the Farnborough Road.

110   Cody's man-lifting kite, *c.*1904.

The army had been using balloons for mapping and surveillance of battle grounds during the latter half of the 19th century and opened their balloon factory at Chatham in 1878. They moved the factory to Aldershot but were soon restricted by the lack of open space. Farnborough, with its wide open areas of common land, was ideally suited and enabled the army to continue its experiments into manned balloon flights. By the time the factory moved to Farnborough a great deal of pioneering work had already been undertaken, in particular by Samuel Franklin Cody, a flamboyant American showman. Cody had come to England in the late 1880s and toured with his own Wild West show, often being mistaken for his namesake 'Buffalo Bill' Cody, of whom he was in fact no relation, but gradually he became more and more interested in kite flying. This had progressed into the development of man-lifting kites and he convinced the army that these would be a good instrument of war.

The first superintendent of the Balloon Factory was Col. Templer, who retired shortly after the move and was replaced by Col. Capper. Although many people were sceptical of Cody's experiments, he found an ally in Col. Capper, who persuaded the army to employ Cody as chief instructor in kite flying at the Balloon Factory. The War Office was still convinced that the way forward lay with the development of airships, and in 1907 Col. Capper and Cody, together with Col. Templer who had been retained as a consultant, oversaw

98

111 Airship *Nulli Secundus II*, a rebuilt version of the first *Nulli Secundus*, flying over the airfield when a summer camp was being held on the common in 1908.

the development of the first British military airship, the *Nulli Secundus*. Together with Lieut. C.M. Waterlow RE, they flew the *Nulli Secundus* the 35 miles to London, but were unable to return because of strong headwinds and had to land at Crystal Palace. Such were the crude beginnings of powered flight experimentation at the Factory.

Col. Templer had for many years been trying to find the ideal material for balloon and airship construction. Eventually an envelope was designed using goldbeater's skin, which was made from the intestines of cattle and oxen bought from local abattoirs. The Weinling family developed a system of cleaning and joining the skins together so the War Office employed them to carry out this rather unpleasant work. For a while, the family did it in their home in Somerset Road and then Miss Weinling became the forewoman of the women workers later employed at the Balloon Factory. The passenger car was suspended below the gas-filled envelope.

Before he took over the Factory, Col. Capper had visited America and met up with the Wright Brothers who had already achieved manned flight in an aeroplane. On his return to England he persuaded the War Office to try to buy one of these aeroplanes but the Wright Brothers did not consider they were ready for marketing. Meanwhile Cody was doggedly struggling to build his own aeroplane and, although he was allowed to work at the Balloon Factory, his experiments had to be funded from his own pocket. Time and again his aeroplane would reach a few feet off the ground, then crash, only to be repaired and wheeled out for a further trial. The people of Farnborough played no small part in these pioneering activities. Many of them would gather on the common to watch and were always ready to give a helping hand if Cody needed it. His determination paid off and in 1908 he was able to record the first powered aeroplane flight in Great Britain. Starting at the Swan end of the airfield, he flew a quarter of a mile in 27 seconds to ensure a well-earned place in aviation history. His experiments had generally received little publicity and, because this flight also ended in a crash, damaging the wings of the aeroplane, the significance of the achievement went almost unheralded in the national press which chose to highlight the crash rather than this first powered flight.

These early flying experiments received much attention from aviation enthusiasts, however. In May 1909 Wilbur Wright, the American air pioneer, and his sister Katherine visited the Balloon Factory as guests of Col. J.E. Capper, and stayed at Col. Capper's house on the corner of Church Road and Alexandra Road. The War Office, though, remained unconvinced and shelved all work on aircraft in favour of further development of airships. The Balloon Factory and Balloon School were divided in that year and Mervyn O'Gorman was made Superintendent of the Factory, where he was instrumental in initiating a more scientific attitude to aeronautical research.

By 1910 the local people were becoming accustomed to seeing huge airships circling the skies of Farnborough. On Wednesday 26 October, Col. Capper had arranged that a new airship, designed by M. Lebaudy, should be flown in from France for trials at the Factory. It had left Moisson in France early in the morning, and five hours later the people of Aldershot and Farnborough were amazed to see an airship that had flown all the way across the Channel. As soon as it came into view, 100 men from the Coldstream Guards' barracks raced up to the common to assist in catching the tow ropes by which method the airship was guided in to land. There was a high wind blowing which made manoeuvring this vast gas-filled bulk all the more difficult. Once it had landed in the marked enclosure, cordoned off by the military police to protect the onlookers, it was steered towards the new airship shed which had been constructed to house it. Unfortunately the builders had underestimated the size of the airship, and as its nose entered the shed its skin snagged a high girder and burst open. The resultant collapse of the whole airship meant that it had to be returned to France for repair. The spectacular flight of the largest

airship ever built in France, over 330 feet in length, was recorded by local photographers and within two days postcards of the event appeared in the local shops.

Before the repaired airship returned to Farnborough in 1911, the shed was raised by an additional 15 feet. This was accomplished by a large force of local workmen, and on 4 May 1911 the *Lebaudy* once again excited the inhabitants as it arrived over the common. High winds again caused a problem. The mooring ropes became loose and dragged the airship across the Farnborough Road to crash into the trees in the garden of Woodlands Cottage, on the corner of Reading Road. The *Lebaudy* did not fly again.

114 Raising the height of the airship shed after the *Lebaudy* airship had been damaged. All the component parts lying on the ground are carefully numbered for insertion into the correct positions.

115 The gang of workmen who raised the roof of the airship shed. Mr. Joe Bedford is standing centre right between the men in light overalls.

That same year, the Balloon Factory became the Army Aircraft Factory. Aircraft design advanced steadily and the first airworthiness certificate was issued and given to the BE1, a biplane designed by Geoffrey de Havilland and F.M. Green. Experiments were also taking place into the design of seaplanes and a few tests were carried out on Cove Reservoir, at the western side of the common. The reservoir was also a very useful leisure facility and local youngsters spent many happy hours swimming there.

By the time Cody died, in a fatal air crash in 1913, the factory had seen another name change to the Royal Aircraft Factory. The Royal Flying Corps had come into being and the Factory was building aeroplanes on a larger scale for both military and civilian use. Greater altitude was being reached, and de

Havilland managed to fly at the dizzy height of over 10,000 feet to gain the altitude record for a British aircraft. A memorial to Cody's achievements at Farnborough is the replica of what is known as Cody's Tree, to which he had tied his earliest aeroplanes when testing their thrust. The original tree stood at the Farnborough end of the runway, but when it died it was replaced by an aluminium replica. This was subsequently moved in 1996 and placed outside the new buildings at the opposite end of the airfield, where the new main gate is called Cody's Gate.

The outbreak of the First World War in 1914 saw a greater concentration on the design and testing of military aircraft. Years of official reluctance to recognise aviation had to be turned around rapidly to cope with the new weapon of war, air power. Hundreds of workers from all over the country were recruited to supplement the local workforce, and by 1916 over 5,000 people were employed, nearly 3,000 of whom were women. This caused great problems to the Council because the influx of workers and their families put quite a strain on local resources. Accommodation was in short supply and the schools suddenly became overcrowded. A small group of cottages, known as Pinehurst Cottages, was constructed on the northern edge of the airfield and this eased the situation. Some of the larger local houses were requisitioned for factory workers' accommodation for the duration of the war. The work involved not only the manufacture of aeroplanes, for much important research was undertaken in the design of all the new instruments needed to fly in war conditions. King George V visited on a number of occasions to inspect the progress and to give encouragement to the work being carried out.

Pioneers such as Cody, Busk, Godden and Keith Lucas have found their way into local road names, along with other high ranking personalities from the Factory such as Perring and Farren. Their names were all familiar to local people. Most of them lived very close by, and at one time all the test pilots lived in Arnold House, a former school, in Southampton Street. The common was accessible to everyone until late into the 1930s, when fences appeared around sensitive areas. The inhabitants of Farnborough in those formative years of flying felt that they too had a place in aviation history. Many families can recount stories from those times of how one or another of their forebears assisted the early aviators to push, pull, restrain or retrieve some form of winged machine. Accidents were numerous and sometimes fatal and it is surprising that not more people were hurt considering how crowded the common became, particularly in the summer.

Another aspect of Factory work, which affected the local community in a different way, was the construction of a railway linking the

116   An army airplane in 1915.

117 Employees in one of the Departments of the RAE in December 1918.

118   The Gates on RAE Railway at the Union Street end of Elm Grove Road. The lines in the road were removed when the railway closed in 1967, but this short stretch of line remains in a grassy patch on the corner.

site to the main railway station. In 1917 it came to the Council's notice that a considerable amount of work had gone into the construction of a railway behind the houses on the southern side of Victoria Road. The Council was anxious to learn the purpose of the new route as it looked as if lines would be laid across Victoria Road and along Elm Grove Road. The War Office confirmed that the railway would be used for transporting fuel to the Factory, but advised the Council that, as the work was in the interests of the war effort, it would be in no position to approve or disapprove of the scheme.

In the event, the War Office gave only one day's notice of its intention to dig up the roads, and that being a Sunday the Council were powerless to muster any physical opposition. The local shopkeepers were none too pleased and bombarded the Council and local newspaper with letters of protest. No compensation was offered for the inconvenience of suddenly having a railway running past the front gates of the cottages in Elm Grove

Road, and the protests continued to be voiced well after the end of hostilities in 1918. Some people tried to claim that their businesses suffered and others that their buildings had been damaged by the constant vibration. It is interesting to note that many of the houses are still standing and the businesses survived successfully until other influences caused their demise. Because the line remained in use in peacetime, the War Office did agree to pay a nominal rent to the Council for using the highway; it also agreed to re-lay the track in Victoria Road because the early lines had been the cause of numerous accidents and were a danger to cyclists. In its early days, the railway engine was always preceded by a man on foot carrying a red flag to warn the traffic. One of the famous engines used was named *Invincible*, and the name remains in Invincible Road which traverses much of the old line. The last journey along the route was in 1967, when *Invincible* was retired to take up duties on the Isle of Wight.

In 1918 the Royal Aircraft Factory was renamed the Royal Aircraft Establishment (RAE) in order to avoid confusion with the newly formed Royal Air Force, itself born out of the Royal Flying Corps, but at the end of the First World War the urgency of the work at the RAE declined and large numbers of staff were laid off. The whole country suffered from an economic depression and government economies dictated heavy cutbacks in aviation research, although some work still continued at Farnborough.

During the First World War, tanks had also made their appearance as a new and effective weapon. In 1921 the Tank Regiment moved into Farnborough and was stationed in Pinehurst Barracks at the edge of the RAE. These huge vehicles became a familiar site

whenever they undertook tests on the common. The roads also suffered and it was very dangerous trying to cross at Pinehurst Corner, at its junction with Farnborough Road, because of the cumbersome vehicles cutting the corners.

On a lighter note, one fond memory of those days is of a very young child singing star called Petula Clark, whose father was based in Farnborough during the Second World War. Petula rose to fame following a concert given to the local troops and so began a career which took her from radio broadcasts during the war to pop singer of the '60s, and on to international stardom.

During the late 1930s attention was focused on the RAE again as the prospect of war loomed on the horizon. A new era in aviation was ahead and the RAE was thronged once again with

119   The *Invincible* railway engine.

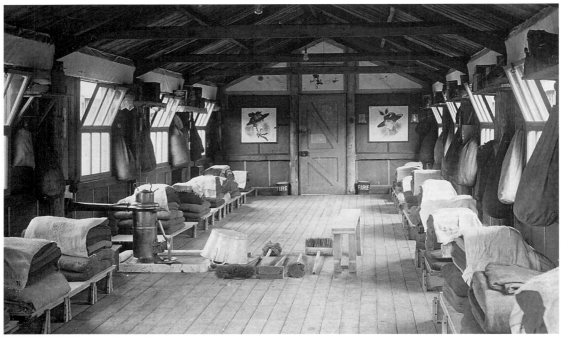

120   Hut 23 at Pinehurst Barracks when used by the Royal Flying Corps during the First World War. No window coverings and a gap under the door must have meant pretty spartan conditions despite the small stove in the centre.

121   The occupants of Hut 23 at Pinehurst Barracks during the First World War.

workers in every field of research imaginable, to ensure the country's superiority in the air. When war broke out in 1939 there were about 500 workers at the RAE, but this number rose rapidly to over 6,000, including about 1,500 research and scientific staff. The research and testing that was undertaken was without parallel and enabled the aircraft industry to manufacture such war-winning aeroplanes as the Lancaster and the Spitfire. Radio, navigation and photograph equipment, as well as gunsights and bombsights, were among the many instruments tested. As well as providing research for our own aircraft industry, other important functions included the examination of captured enemy equipment. After the war ended in 1945, all the captured enemy

aircraft were put on display before an invited crowd, which included families of the employees who had worked on them.

Three years later, the Society of British Aircraft Constructors moved its annual air show to Farnborough. For nearly half a century, the skies of Farnborough had echoed to the sounds of experimental flying, so where the country was still dragging itself out of post-war austerity here was a chance for the British aircraft industry to show off its developing jets and prototype airliners. Britain was looking for exports and Farnborough became a place for the world to see how aviation had advanced since those early days when Cody experimented with man-lifting kites.

122   King George V and Queen Mary visiting the School of Photography.

123   The Brabazon airliner flew over the town before landing at the airshow in 1950. At the time it was the largest airliner in the world, so large that it could not turn round on the runway but had to be towed back along it before it could take off. Cody's tree is in the fenced off area.

The first jet airliners were appearing, and a few days before the show John Derry became the first British pilot to break the Sound Barrier. The public was allowed in at the weekend for the first time at such a show, and nearly 150,000 visitors came to be thrilled by the air displays. Thousands of cars and coaches poured into the town and special trains were laid on with shuttle bus services running from all the local stations. The following year, it was estimated that more than 300,000 saw the show. Each year the crowds grew larger and brought with them the now familiar traffic jams. At various times during the day the local roads became totally congested. In 1950 the local paper reported stationary traffic from Farnham Wharf Bridge to Frimley and in 1951, on one of the public days, traffic tailed back as far as Bagshot. Since 1962 the event has become bi-annual, but there are still traffic jams when the crowds flock to what is now called Farnborough International.

The early days of experimental flying saw some fatalities, and tragedy struck the airshow in 1952 when a DH 110 broke up and crashed, killing the pilot, John Derry, and his observer, Tony Richards. An engine rolled into the crowd killing and injuring more spectators. In 1968 a French aircraft crashed into some workshops near the Farnborough Road. The tail section ended up embedded in the senior staff mess which, miraculously, was empty at the time. Six people died, including the crew of the aircraft and one RAE employee.

Research and planning for future developments in the industry has always been the core element of the RAE. In the 1950s and 1960s much new equipment was constructed to cope with the demand for testing ever bigger, better and faster aircraft. In 1966 the Queen and the Duke of Edinburgh visited the RAE to open a new multi-million pound structure-testing facility. As the world moved into the supersonic age, the RAE at Farnborough moved with it.

At the 1970 airshow, Concorde, the world's fastest airliner, made its first spectacular

124   Visitors to the airshow crossing the Farnborough Road via a temporary bridge in 1966. A temporary bridge has been put up for each successive airshow.

125 Heavy equipment was brought in to remove the crashed aircraft in 1968. As the inquiry into the cause of the crash got underway, the RAE appealed for any photographs from the public which might help with their investigations.

126 Concorde flew over the Clockhouse when it made its first appearance at Farnborough in 1970.

public appearance. The crowds marvelled that such a beautiful aircraft, which could attain supersonic speeds, could also fly so slowly and gracefully over the airfield.

Structure tests were still being carried out on the airliner, and huge sections of another early Concorde were transported by lorry at a much more modest speed. Oversize lorries carrying mysteriously shaped loads covered in tarpaulin and heading for the RAE were a not uncommon sight on the local roads, and occasionally they caused traffic disruption. But when Concorde came to town in September 1970 it was a major logistical exercise to move one of the largest loads ever seen in Surrey and Hampshire. Three giant Pickford's lorries travelled from Southampton up the A30 to Blackbushe, where they stayed overnight. Early

next morning they commenced the three-hour crawl to the RAE, travelling via the newly constructed but as yet unopened section of the M3 motorway from Lightwater to the Hawley Lane Junction. Special ramps were constructed to allow the 25 ft. wide loads to descend from the motorway, which then continued their ponderous journey along the Farnborough Road. The Council had to trim trees, dismantle road signs, pull out bollards and even remove the traffic lights at the RAE to allow the convoy to pass.

The RAE became DERA and is now part of QinetiQ and has moved to the other end of the airfield. Current development of the old Factory site and the plans for the airfield seem set to ensure that Farnborough retains its venerable links with aviation history.

127   A giant Pickford's transporter travelling past *The Ship*, taking parts of Concorde to the RAE for structure testing.

Chapter Nine

Beneath the Wings

Whilst Farnborough was becoming the focus for aviation development, the local inhabitants were busy going about their daily life. More and more people were obtaining employment at the Balloon Factory, although 'going into service' in the big houses was still the major option for young women. It was the onset of the First World War that really brought about the first major changes for women. Thousands of men joined up to serve their country, leaving families behind to carry on working in the essential services.

Farnborough Post Office took on a number of post girls to deliver the mail. One

128   Mr. Algernon Collins' shop on the Farnborough Road, near the *Queen's Hotel*, was popular with the men of the Royal Flying Corps, whose headquarters were on the opposite side of the road. Blowes, in Aero House on the right, became the Aero Café.

129   Post girls during the First World War. Miss Helen (Nellie) Hockley is standing on the far right.

130   Certificate presented to local men who had served in the First World War.

of these, young Nellie Hockley, had the sad task of delivering a telegram to her mother, advising of the death of a soldier son. Such was the confusion as the terrible battles raged across Europe that information was not always accurate. Fortunately, in this case, Bert Hockley was discovered to be alive, as a prisoner of war, and he survived to return home. All former prisoners of war received a letter from the King, and Mr. Hockley also received a certificate of gratitude from the people of Farnborough.

Aviation was in the blood of many of the local youngsters, who were eager to join the Royal Flying Corps, the forerunner of the Royal Air Force. A special memorial to those who perished was established in the Lady Chapel

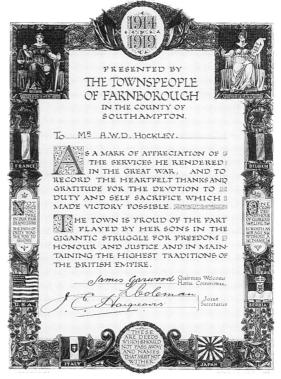

131   Jubilee Hall Club officers and committee, 1924-5. From left to right, front row: R.D. McLaurin, A.E. Lovegrove, A.G. Every, L. Coleman, G.E. Dew; second row: W.A. Chalk, G. Lloyd, J.K. Jacques, G. Lancaster, A.T. Hammond, H. Lancaster; back row: F. Paice, W.R. Weller.

of St Mark's Church after the war. The walls of the chapel are lined with oak panelling inscribed with the names of servicemen who died in both the world wars. The Farnborough and Cove Cottage Hospital in Albert Road was established in a house purchased by the townspeople of Farnborough and Cove as a memorial to the First World War dead. It is now called Devereux House and is part of a sheltered care facility. After the Second World War, Knellwood House came on the market and that was converted into the Farnborough and Cove War Memorial Residential Home for the Elderly.

In the early part of the 20th century a number of social clubs were formed, and a very popular one was the Jubilee Hall Club.

The Hall, erected in 1897 to celebrate Queen Victoria's Diamond Jubilee, was on land near Farnborough Station donated by Joseph Holt of Farnborough Grange. It was used for parish and community events and the club continues to this day, but it had to relocate when the Hall was demolished in the 1970s.

South Farnborough had the Working Men's Club in York Road and the Social Club in Peabody Road. These clubs gave people the opportunity to participate in social activities which they could not do at home. There was no TV in most homes until the late 1950s, nor did many families drive their own motor cars. So trips to places of interest were often organised, when picnics would be enjoyed along with the simple pleasures of walking and playing in the countryside. It is hard to imagine today, with our air-conditioned, seat-belted luxury coaches, how the first day trippers fared in their open-top, wooden-seated charabancs. The local paper reported on one group of local residents who braved the journey to Calais and back in one day in 1906. Day trips to Cherbourg were also advertised.

The large number of people employed at the RAE also formed themselves into numerous social clubs for a variety of activities. One of the most successful and enduring has been the Operatic Society. Like most of the RAE clubs, it opened up its doors to those who did not work there, but it retained the connection in the name which currently is the DERA Farnborough Amateur Operatic Society.

The youngsters of the town were eager to become involved in the new Boy Scouts and Girl Guides movements. Lord Baden-Powell, their founder, had served locally in the army and many rallies took place on the Aldershot Parade Ground. As early as 1908, Miss E.D. Vinson, a local school teacher, started to organise a group of guides. Early meetings were held in the grounds of St Mark's Vicarage.

For a very short period just before the Second World War local people were able to enjoy the fun of a miniature railway. In 1936 Mr. Charles Bullock, who lived at 'The Olives'

in Prospect Road, built a miniature railway just across the road on land near the Grammar School he leased from Mr. Ratcliffe. It was near a public footpath and, although originally built for his own amusement, soon attracted public attention. Mr. Bullock was joined in his venture by Dr. Alexander Davenport Kinloch, and they opened it to the public in June of the same year. Thousands of people took rides on the miniature trains, which stopped at a number of small stations on a line that eventually ran from Farnborough Green to Fox Hills. There were five platforms at the terminus at Farnborough Green which made it the largest miniature railway terminus ever constructed. It closed in September 1939 on the outbreak of war and was eventually dismantled.

Once again the nation was engaged in conflict. With the military presence so close in Aldershot and the sensitive nature of the work at the RAE, it was felt the area might well be a target for enemy action. The first air-raid sirens sounded locally in the early days of September but they were only warnings. Preparations were made for possible raids but, while many parts of the country suffered terrible ordeals, Farnborough remained relatively unscathed. A diary kept by one of the nuns at Farnborough Hill Convent describes some days of continuous overhead activity and endless

132 The pupils of the Salesian School are waiting for the charabancs to leave on an outing to Littlehampton as they celebrate Rectors Day in 1926.

133   5th Farnborough Scouts in the 1930s.

134   An engine on the turntable at the Farnborough Miniature Railway, 1937.

135 Red Cross and Civil Defence workers at the Castleden Hall first-aid post and ambulance depot during the Second World War.

nights when the sky was lit up by searchlights in the distance. From their position on the hill, they could see the glow of fires in the distance. When London was being bombed, the planes droned over in waves. The diary recounts how the pupils were nearly shot out of bed by the noise of the first bombs being dropped at nearby Frimley Green, the trips to the shelters which had been constructed, often two or three times a night, the thuds and explosions from distant bombing, and the relief when the all-clear was sounded.

In August 1940 Farnborough received its first air raid. Eight enemy aircraft flew in low across the airfield dropping a number of bombs on the RAE and on the residential area to the east of the Farnborough Road. There were three fatalities in the RAE and a number of injuries. One house was demolished in Albert Road,

damage was caused to nearby houses, including the cottage hospital, and a delayed action bomb landed in a garden on the corner of Canterbury and Cambridge Roads. Civil Defence services sprang into well co-ordinated action and the casualties were attended to within minutes. They were taken to the first-aid post at Castleden Hall, where a temporary mortuary had also been set up. Many people had used the public shelters while the raid was on, and next day nearby residents were temporarily evacuated whilst the Royal Engineers dealt with the unexploded bomb. This was the first test for the emergency services and in a subsequent report to the Council the Chief Executive Officer felt that the preparations had been quite adequate.

The local people were well prepared. Many had enrolled in the Civil Defence as air-raid wardens and fire watchers. The streets

136   Wartime Salvage Parade in Alexandra Road in 1942.

137   *Ridgemont Hotel, c.1940s.*

were patrolled during darkness to ensure that the blacked-out windows did not let through even the tiny chink of light which could attract attention from the air. Rest Centres were set up but, as people were often reluctant to attend them, a 'Good Neighbour' scheme was instituted by the Women's Voluntary Service, whereby people made homeless would be temporarily billeted with neighbours until suitable accommodation could be found for them. The efforts of the Civil Defence and WVS were unceasing and undoubtedly helped to bring people through six difficult years of war.

Despite the disruption of the air-raid warnings, and occasional raids resulting in some fatalities and injuries, the inhabitants put their minds to supporting the war effort. All spare land was used for growing vegetables, the Council provided special kerbside bins for the collection of food scraps which could be used to feed pigs, waste paper was collected on a vast scale, and competitions were held to see which schools could collect the most scrap iron. The Ministry of Supply was very impressed with Farnborough's efforts and encouraged other Councils to follow their example. To get the message over to the townspeople, the Council organised a big parade in 1942 to show what could be collected and how it could be used.

Tearooms were popular meeting places until coffee bars opened up in the 1950s. The *Ridgemont Hotel*, now the *Falcon*, opposite the RAE on Aircraft Esplanade, was ideally positioned to attract both local and passing trade. It was open on Sundays and had a Tea Lounge as well as a restaurant.

People still had time to enjoy themselves and dancing was very popular, particularly while the Canadian troops were in the camp. They had money and could afford to take the girls out to the cinemas or dance halls. Dances were held in the Town Hall or at 'The Bucket of Blood' in Queen's Road, so nicknamed because of the rather vicious fights between the Canadians and the local lads, usually over the girls. Now home to a dancing school, the building was originally

a Mission Hall and during the First World War had been a soldiers' club.

At the end of the war came wild celebrations. There were victory parades, thanksgiving services, dances and dozens of street parties. Somehow the organisers managed to produce party food which had been so restricted during the conflict. Even though food rationing continued for some years after the war, such luxuries as mince pies, jellies, doughnuts, and loads of sandwiches managed to find their way to the gaily decorated tables. It was the first time many children had ever seen such goodies.

The popularity of dancing brought about the formation of a number of small bands. A popular group which emerged in the late 1940s was called the Rhythm Swingtet and it used to practise regularly in the hall at Queen's Road School. The headmaster, Mr. Charlton, was a keen supporter of the band, and allowed them to use the school without charge. In return they often played at the 14/20 Youth Club dances which had previously had to make do with gramophone records.

There were still two cinemas in the town, the Scala in Camp Road, and the Rex, on the Farnborough Road near the *Tumbledown Dick*. The Rex had been opened in 1937 by film star Jesse Matthews. It had taken local builder, Mr. J. Chuter, only four months to construct and boasted the most modern sound and projection equipment in the country. 'Mirrorphonic Sound' was proclaimed to 'reproduce every individual characteristic of speech in such a clear and precise manner that nowhere in the auditorium could it not be heard'. With the advent of television, cinemas gradually went into decline and the Rex was eventually pulled down in the 1970s to make way for the Kingsmead shopping complex.

Big estates were springing up to the north and west of the town and the military presence in North Camp was dwindling. Although North Camp had been considered the best shopping area for miles around, it was now felt necessary to provide shopping facilities in a more central

138   Queen's Road VE Day party, 1945.

position. In the late 1950s building commenced on a new shopping centre to the west of the Clockhouse, off Victoria Road. Two large houses, Queensmead and Kingsmead, were demolished to make way for the entrance, and the complex was subsequently extended into Princes Mead. Modern shopping habits have taken people to out-of-town stores, but as we go into the 21st century work has already started on the regeneration of this town centre shopping area.

The 1950s brought the coronation of Queen Elizabeth II and a general feeling that the country was moving towards a brighter future. Shops and buildings were festooned with flags and street parties were held all over the town. The Town Hall decorations were flood-lit and all the roadside flower beds were ablaze with red, white and blue flowers. The austerity of the previous decade gradually gave way to increased prosperity. A new estate was constructed to the north-west of the town to house a large number of people being moved out of London. New private houses were built, more jobs were created, and labour-saving goods and televisions started to appear in the home. The motor car was becoming more affordable, which brought increased traffic on the roads. A roundabout at the Clockhouse was one answer to ease the congestion at this busy six-way crossroads. It is still a congested area and the size of this roundabout constantly

139   Rhythm Swingtet in 1948. Left to right: Mr. Charlton, headmaster of Queen's Road School, 'Finn' Lawlor (piano), Peter Maher (guitar), Peter Holman (trumpet), Denys Watmore (saxophone), John Holman (saxophone) and Ron 'Jumbo' Howlett (drums).

140   The Rex cinema in the 1970s, when its popularity was in decline.

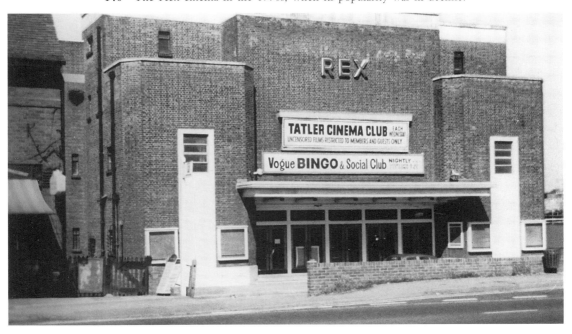

141   Somerset Road Coronation street party held in the St John Ambulance Hall in 1953.

changes as different theories about traffic control are put to the test. Today it is less than half its original size but takes two lanes of traffic from all directions.

The 1960s were a decade of freedom and people power, when protesters took part in huge marches around the country to support various causes. There was one problem which drove the respectable people of Farnborough to take up their placards in desperation—and that was coal! Not the lack of it but dust from the huge quantities piled high in the coal yards at Farnborough Station. Clouds of dust were blowing into the houses in Union Street, making washing dirty and creating a health hazard. The residents found support from the rector's wife and other ladies of the church who marched with the residents through Queensmead in May 1966 to the clanging of an old school bell. The protest caught the eye of the national press and the *Express* reported that 'Police held up the traffic as the procession of wives with 10 prams and a dog

142   Rumble's shop advertising state of the art refrigerator in 1953.

143   Clockhouse roundabout, *c.*1951.

144 Coal Dust march, Queensmead, 1966. Mrs. Betty Hutchinson leads the protesters, followed by Mrs. Maston, Mrs. Railton, Mrs. Hobday, Mrs. Frieze-Green, Mrs. Walker Briggs and Mrs. Rutland.

145 Following the protest, this 18ft. high protective fence was erected between the coal yard and Union Street.

made for the coal depot'. The coal company was supposed to plant a screen of trees to alleviate the problem but in the end they were forced to erect a huge fence over 18ft. foot high.

Summer days always seemed to be full of sunshine in times gone by. Certainly the outdoor swimming pool, affectionately called 'The Puddle', was well used. It was built in the grounds of Castleden Hall, on Boundary Road, and on a hot summer's day was always crowded. It eventually closed with the redevelopment of the land for the College of Technology but the Recreation Centre on Meudon Avenue now provides very good swimming facilities.

Farnborough Urban District Council administered the town through the first quarter of the century, but during the 1920s there was much talk about amalgamating with Aldershot or Cove. At that time local issues were considered more important than political persuasion in Council elections, but at one election in 1928 only 25 per cent of those eligible bothered to cast a vote. Eventually, in 1932, amalgamation with Cove and parts of Hawley gave the Council a much larger area to govern. Local government re-organisation in 1974 saw amalgamation with Aldershot to form the Borough of Rushmoor, which body has managed local affairs ever since. The heritage of Farnborough lives on in the Borough's Coat of Arms, which incorporates a key surmounted by an Astral Crown to represent the RAE, and the original ferns of Ferneberga.

146　'The Puddle' swimming pool in the summer of 1970.

FARNBOROUGH URBAN DISTRICT
COUNCIL ELECTION, 1928

POLLING DAY:
Monday, April 2nd.

Study Your Interests
AND VOTE FOR
BARTON

147 Mr. Barton, an estate agent from North Camp, stood in the Council election in 1928.

148 Rushmoor Coat of Arms.

STRENGTH IN UNITY

Index

Pages on which illustrations appear are shown in **bold** type